Intuitive
C++

An Introduction for C Programmers

Ann Weintz

Includes
X Window System and NeXT examples
and
Instructions for getting free GNU C++

Intuitive C++

Other Books by Ann Weintz
_____

Writing NeXT Programs

Chapter One
Creating A Trivial Object

The C++ programming language is neither difficult nor complicated. In fact, for the C programmer, it is exactly the opposite. Most features of C++ can be viewed as natural extensions of the C language, and are really intuitive when viewed from the right perspective.

The intent of this book is to help the reader see the natural simplicity of the language. We will start out by using the most powerful new feature of C++: A feature which is the basis of a new technique called "Object Oriented Programming."

The first "trivial" example we will try is only fifteen lines of code, but it illustrates the essential power of C++.

C++ allows programs to be structured in a totally new way, and also allows problems to be looked at from a new perspective. So, although this first example is trivial in size and complexity, don't underestimate its power.

It will take the entire Chapter to write the fifteen lines of code. That is because we are going to get a first exposure to the language, and time is required to feel comfortable with the concept of programing with objects.

A Few Assumptions

Unlike most books, this book will look at C++ from the perspective of the way memory is used. Practically speaking, both C and C++ require an understanding of the underlying machine which is being used. That is because both C and C++ use pointers, stack variables, and memory. Since memory can be directly accessed, the programmer must understand the size of addresses and memory. Otherwise it is impossible to choose a variable of the correct size to reference memory, or to adjust values at offsets from a specified address.

Most programmers are using a machine which has a four byte integer at a four byte address, so we will use those sizes in our examples.

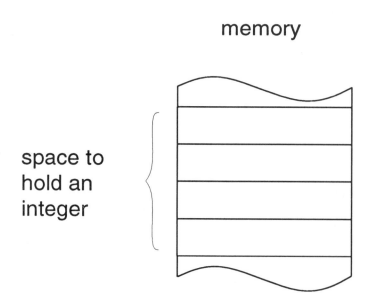

memory

space to hold an integer

Integers and Addresses are four bytes

Of course, on some machines this won't be true. Some early IBM PCs, for example, still use two byte integers and either two or four byte addresses. Those few readers with unusual word or address sizes will need to mentally adjust the descriptions given in this book.

A Closer Look at C

Since the new features of C++ can be viewed as natural extensions of C, we will start by reviewing some portions of C. We will then introduce our trivial example by explaining how it differs from C.

In the C programming language, someone had an idea:

There is something called an "int" in C which automatically makes the compiler allocate space for a number.

The "int" keyword allows a programmer to use integers at any time in a program, and for any duration. To anyone who has programmed for a while, this should seem very obvious: Every language has the concept of a variable.

What is significant is how C++ uses this idea. Just as C uses the type "int" to represent a number, C++ will define a new type to represent "objects."

Before we can look at objects, though, we've got to examine a few more characteristics of the C language.

Each time a programmer defines an integer, memory space is allocated for that integer. And, in general, four bytes are allocated for an integer variable.

memory

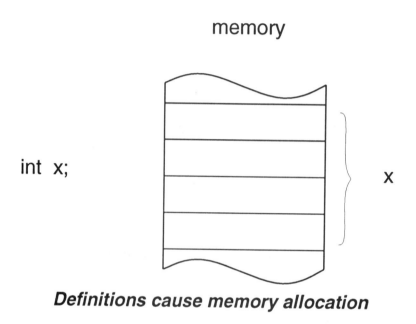

int x;

x

Definitions cause memory allocation

But the inventors of the C language didn't stop with the definition of an "int." They had another idea:

We can let C programmers initialize the variable at the same time they allocate memory space for the variable.

Of course, this is simply common programming practice. This feature is used in this way.

memory

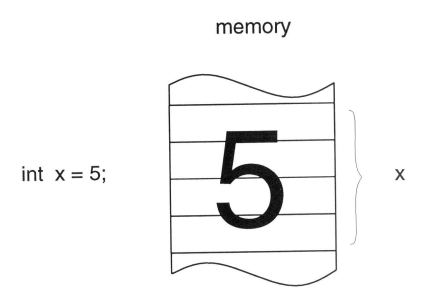

int x = 5;

This statement actually does two things. It first allocates space for our new variable type (a four byte integer), and then puts the number five into those four bytes.

You are probably wondering why we are reviewing these features of C. I've no doubt that we are all very familiar with defining integers. And, in fact, it would be hard to write a progam without defining integers.

But that is exactly the point. *We are going from a language which is built around using variables to a language which is built around using objects.* We will soon find it difficult to write a program without defining objects. And an object is simply a new type; just as an integer is a type. And just as we can both allocate space for integers and initialize integers, we will soon be allocating and initializing objects.

Before we start working with objects in C++, we need to review some more C. Here is another good observation to make about C.

In C, we allow programmers to use the keyword "int" over and over: And each time we use the keyword, the compiler allocates space for another number. And, we allow programmers to initialize the data, too!

Again, we are just reviewing standard C. In practice, this looks like:

memory

int x = 5;
int y = 3;
int z = 2;

C allows memory allocation and initialization

Ok. We now have a good background to understand the basic C extensions for Object Oriented Programming.

So what about C++?

Well, not to be outdone, the inventors of C++ had some bright ideas too. This one is the most important.

In C, programmers have a way to allocate and initialize data space. So why stop now??

Why not give programmers a keyword which will allocate space for a bunch of code? And the programmer can initialize that space with any set of code he wants!

Lets call the "bunch of code" an object!

This is a fundamental idea of Object Oriented Programming. An object oriented language allows a "bunch of code" to be treated as a single entity. This is analagous to C, which allows a "number" to be treated as a single entity.

In C, we have the type "int", which represents a number. We will soon be looking at a new keyword in C++ which represents a "bunch of code."

To get a better idea of this concept, we have an example which is *not* real code. It is pseudocode. This gives the *idea* of our new keyword.

memory

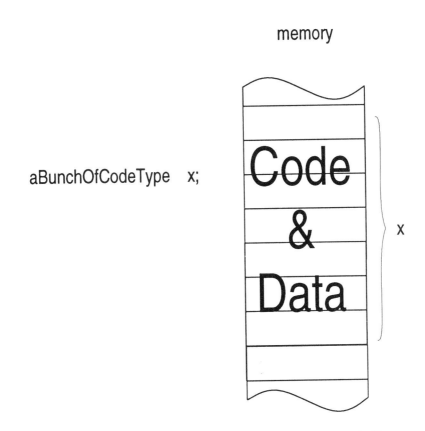

aBunchOfCodeType   x;

C++ has a type for "aBunchofCode"

As you can see this is really the same thing as defining an integer. We simply define a variable of our new type. But, unlike C, the variable refers to a set of functions and associated data.

So, our new type just happens to have C++ code and data. And that code and data get put into memory when we define the type.

This is similar to C, where a statement such as:

```
int x = 5;
```

causes the number five to be put into memory. Except that in C++, we can have functions put into memory instead of a simple number.

We still have a lot to look at, though, before we can actually use this new feature. In particular, there is one major problem to get around.

How can this new type, which represents "a bunch of code," be specified??

As you probably guessed, there is a solution to this problem.

We need to "group" a set of functions and a set of variables together, so that they represent our "bunch of code."

Hmmm.....

This sounds very similar to a typical C structure. After all, a structure typically groups data of different types. We just need to allow code to be added to a structure.

This observation turns out to be very useful. Since a "struct" does something similar to what we want an object to do, we can probably just modify the "struct" syntax.

A typical C structure looks like:

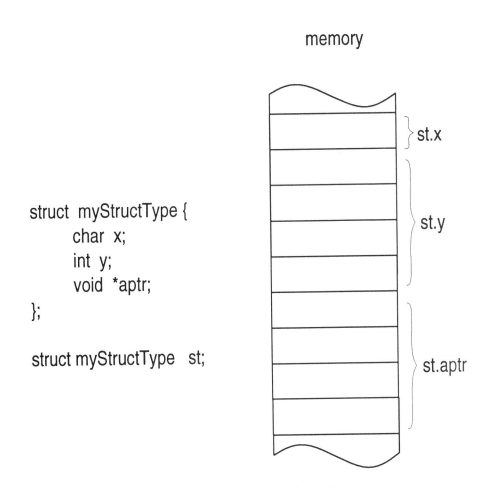

A C structure groups data types.

I hope that the use of struct's is clear. If not, I strongly recommend that you review them. There are many good introductory books on C. (The Waite Group's C Primer Plus is an excellent tutorial.)

So, now we know that objects are collections of C code, just as structures are collections of variables. If you are confused about structures, you will be *more* confused about objects: Since objects are much more flexible, and have all the functionality of structures as a subset of their capabilities.

So, our new "grouping" type for C++ code and data will be a modified structure type. But we can't call it a structure, since C already uses the "struct" keyword.

Let's call our new type a "class."

So we suddenly have a new type. And rather than use the word "struct," we use the word class. Although this keyword provides essentially the same functionality as a structure, it is an *extension* to the language, so it also adds new functionality. The type "class" also differs from structures in some subtle ways. We will be examing the differences soon. Our new syntax looks like:

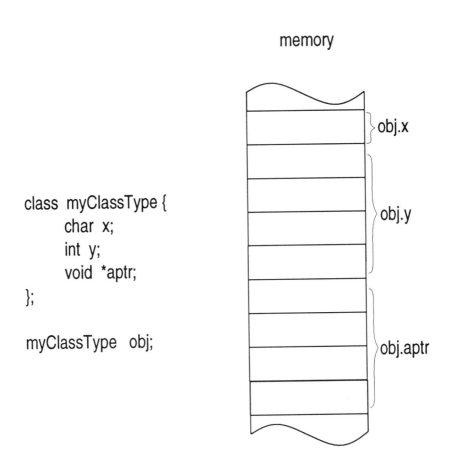

C++ "class" type is like a structure

You've probably noticed that the syntax is almost identical to the syntax used for a structure. The major difference is the word "class" rather than the word "struct".

Another difference is the last line, where we wrote:

```
myClassType obj;
```

rather than

```
class myClassType obj;
```

We were able to skip the keyword "class" because a class is automatically made a type.

And, just as a struct lets you create variables of the type of the structure, a class definition lets you create objects with the type of the class.

That is, in C, you declare a struct:

```
struct mystruct{
    int a;
    char b;
}

struct mystruct astruct;
```

We can call `astruct` an instance of the structure type `mystruct`. Similarly,

```
class myclass {
    int a;
    char b;
}

class myclass anObject;
```

We could call `anObject` an instance of the type `myclass`.

This is typical terminology. A class defines the code and data. An object is an instance of the class, which we can then subsequently use and modify in our running program.

A class has been likened to a cookie cutter. A cookie cutter is not a cookie. It is used to create cookies. Similarly, a class is not an object. A class is used to create objects. Objects are instances of code and data in your running program.

The keyword "class" indicates to the compiler that this variable type is allowed include code and data. In particular, functions can be included in a class definition.

So we have a new syntax. And we can make it work like a "struct." We can use "dots" and "arrows" to access elements of our class.

So, if we have a pointer to an object, we can refer to a variable it contains using:

```
anObject->a;            /* member a of anObject */
```

or, in order to call a function which is in that object, we would use:

```
anObject->afunc();      /* call afunc() in anObject */
```

So we can "steal" the syntax of structures in order to reference code and data in a class.

15

Of course, this doesn't do us much good until we define a new way to get code into our class.

After all, the whole idea is to create a new type which represents both code and data.

The idea is simple: Just as data can be referenced in a structure or class, allow a function to be referenced from a class definition.

We simply add a function reference to our standard "struct". An example which adds the code of "afunc()" to a class is:

memory

```
class myClassType {
      int  x;
      int  afunc();
};

myClassType  anObj;
```

Code (afunc) & Data (x)

} anObj

A class allows functions to be included.

By the way, this code sample is not compilable, since we don't define the function that we reference. Other than that, the code is valid.

There is still one more "trick" to learn before we can create our working C++ program. The "trick" is the correct way to declare functions which are associated with a class.

You may wonder why a function declaration for a class would be any different than regular ANSI C. Well, the reason is that two classes may have a function of the same name. Although this may seem confusing, it is really an essential feature.

For example, if you created a class which provides the status of your disk drive, and another class which gives you the status of your display, you would want to invoke both of those functions using the same name: status.

That is, you might invoke each using:

```
myDiskObj.status()
myDisplayObj.status();
```

Of course, the code which is called as a result of these function calls must be very different. The status() function for a disk is much different from the status() function for a display device.

This means that we need some way to associate a function with a particular class.

***So our previous declaration of the class is
incomplete. It is incomplete because we did***

not specify the code of "afunc()".

When specifying the code of "afunc()", we must be sure that the compiler knows to group it with our new class, "myClassType".

We tell the compiler to associate it with our class by using the new C++ operator "::".

The :: symbol allows the programmer to assocate a variable with a specific class. An example of its use is:

memory

```
class  myClassType {
        int  x;
        int  afunc();
};

myClassType::afunc()
{
        printf("Hi\n");
}

myClassType  anObj;
```

Code
(afunc)
&
Data
(x)

} anObj

The :: associates our function with our class

The :: operator is considered a scoping operator. It defines the scope
for a variable or a function. We will use this operator often in C++,
since it is often desirable to have functions of the same name associated with different objects.

Unfortunately, our code still doesn't do anything useful. In spite of all the work we've done creating our C++ class, there is still another problem with our code...

The code we just looked at won't work. That is because of an important difference between a class and a structure.

A structure, by default, lets anyone access its members.

A class, by default, lets no one access its members.

That is, by definition, all members of a class are private. That means that they can't be accessed by any code outside of the class itself. In the trivial code we have so far, we have no way to invoke any functions in the class. Obviously, there must be a simple solution. (Otherwise all this C++ stuff would be pretty useless.)

There is a new keyword which specifes that a class member can be accessed by anyone. That is the "public" keyword. It is used like this:

memory

```
class myClassType {
public:
      int x;
      int afunc();
};

myClassType::afunc()
{
      printf("Hi\n");
}

myClassType anObj;
```

Use "public" to allow member access

Any variables or functions which follow the keyword "public" can be accessed by anyone. That means that, in the example above, both x and afunc() can be referenced by any other code.

An Important Detail

Although we have been viewing objects as "modified structures," there are some important differences between them.

In this chapter, we will not be too concerned about them, but I do want to modify our "visualization" of an object. Previously, I've depicted objects as being contiguous in memory. That is, I've shown the code and data to be together. In reality, the code and data are often separated.

Misleading!

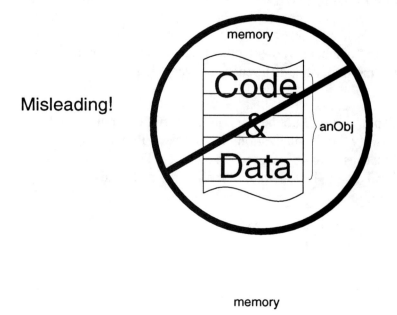

Right!

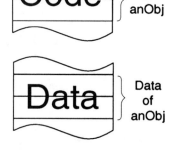

An Object hides pointers to its functions

So what? Well, there are some significant differences when pointers
to objects are involved.

For example, when using structures we are probably accustomed to using data which is contiguous in memory. This means that a structure member which is referenced using a "dot" is simply accessed by adding a fixed offset to the structure's starting address.

That is not true of objects. If you have a pointer to an object, and assume that functions are at fixed offsets from that pointer, your code will not work.

Instead, objects keep information about their functions, and use a hidden mechanism to make it appear as though a "dot" simply points at the correct function.

This will be even more significant when we examine modifying existing objects. *Since objects keep information about the functions they contain, an object can intentionally "branch" you to a function which you don't expect.* Although this sounds confusing now, this will turn out to be a very useful feature of Object Oriented Programming.

And, when someone gives you an object which calls a function, *you will be able to make the object call your function instead.* So, it is this separation of code and data which allows a "jump table" to be inserted into an object, and thereby makes objects modifiable.

The Trivial Example

We finally made it. We are now able to create an Object Oriented Program in C++.

```
class myClassType{
```

```
public:
   int x;
   int afunc();
};

myClassType::afunc()
{
   printf("in afunc\n");
}

main()
{
   myClassType anObj;
   anObj.afunc();   /* call afunc() */
}
```

Getting this code compiled

Unfortunatey, each compiler vendor seems to have unique command line options and "incantations" to invoke their compiler.

In the body of the book I'll give the commands used to compile with the GNU public domain compiler, which is available free from the Free Software Foundation. I'm running the version which is supplied on the NeXT computer. Instructions for getting the full source to the compiler can be found in the appendix.

I entered the above source code into a file called trivial.c, and typed the following command.

cc++ trivial.c

I got a warning, since I didn't declare the function `printf()` before I used it. But the program runs.

In general, C++ expects you to declare functions before their use.

If your compiler complains about the use of `printf()`, it is probably because `printf()` is not a standard part of C++. In general, it is provided by the compiler vendors, but you may have to hunt for it in a library.

C++ has a new, object based I/O system. If you don't have `printf()` you might check the "Miscellaneous Features" chapter to get some basics of C++ I/O.

About C++

If you stop reading this book now, you will already have the most important new concept for programming in the next decade: Modularizing your program into reusable groups of code.

Viewing a program as a collection of reusable objects allows a level of modularity which has never been possible before.

Imagine a drawing tool object which is designed to operate on a window object. You would be able to dynamically create that drawing tool object and specify a window which it should operate on. Regardless of whether that window contained text, data, or 3D graphics! Of course, there is the underlying assumption that the window object has a standard structure which all objects understand.

Suddenly, it is possible to create complex programs by mixing and matching objects.

Still, we have quite a bit to learn about objects. We haven't yet seen how we can combine and modify existing objects. In later chapters, we will see that it is possible to substitute functions in an existing object. This will allow you to take someone's object and modify it for your own use.

Chapter Two
A Better Pointer??

In this Chapter we will be looking at a new feature of C++: A feature which is very similar to the traditional C pointer.

This new feature is called a "reference," and is a new type of variable. This new type is similar to a pointer, but is not similar enough to be able to replace the pointer type. That means that we have a new variable type whose use is subtly different from pointers, yet we will still use pointers.

This "reference" type is commonly used with objects, since it adds some efficiency to their use. So, we will need to understand it both to use it in our own code, as well as to use objects which are created by others.

Like the last Chapter, we will start by reviewing some basic characteristics of the C language so that we can understand some of the subtle characteristics of this new type.

A Closer Look at C

In the last chapter, we started out by looking at a simple declaration of an integer. We will do the same again in this Chapter. Like the last Chapter, this may seem like a long review: But, again like last chapter, the concepts which will be reviewed were specifically chosen because they relate so closely to new features of C++.

In the last Chapter, we saw that the "int" keyword allows a programmer to use integers at any time in a program, and for any duration.

A definition of the form:

int x = 5;

Will cause memory space to be allocated for an integer type. This memory will typically occupy four contiguous bytes.

On all popular machines, each byte has an address. That means that a typical integer variable will be placed in a range of bytes that has four addresses associated with it.

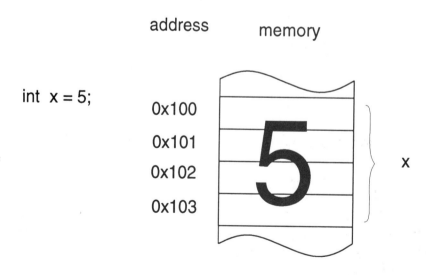

Variables have addresses

In the diagram above, our integer "5" spans the four addresses 0x100, 0x101, 0x102, and 0x103.

In ANSI C, there is an "address" operator, "&", which will give the address of a variable. If we use the "address" operator on our integer variable, the compiler will give us the lowest address of the four byte range: In this case, 0x100.

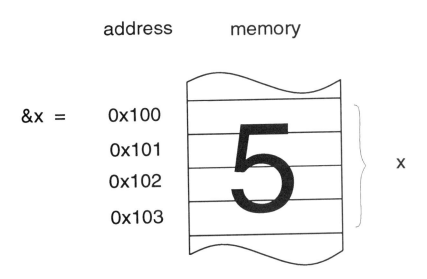

A single address represents the variable

Practically speaking, the number "5" itself would be placed in only one of the bytes, while the other bytes are empty. Of course, if we stored a larger number, more of the bytes would be used. In any case, the address operator would only give the address of the lowest byte in the four byte set.

Interestingly, an address is normally, and intuitively, a location for a byte, by the very design of the machine. So there are, in reality, four bytes in the address of our integer.

Yet, when we ask the compiler for the address of our integer, it returns a single byte address. That is because the compiler knows that an integer variable will occupy four bytes. And, when we use that single address to refer to an integer, the compiler will automatically use all four bytes.

So the C compiler is accessing a range of addresses in a non-intuitive manner, based on the fact that we define the space for an integer. We will soon see C++ making some similarly non-intuitive use of addresses.

In the case of

```
int x = 5;
```

we can also put that address into another variable, using a statement such as:

```
int *y = &x;
```

In other words,

It is also possible to have a variable whose contents is an address.
These are usually called "pointers," since

they "point" to where some useful data is kept.

Of course, every C programmer knows this. And it is done in the typical manner:

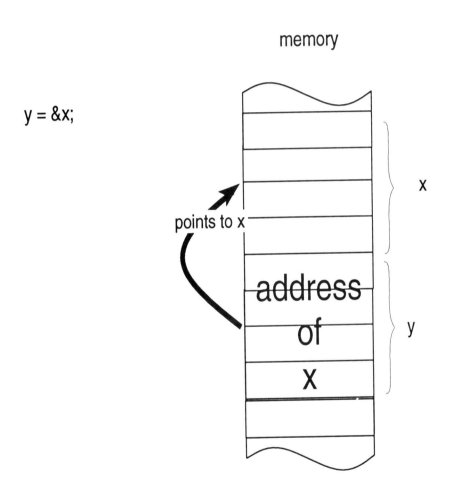

A pointer is an address

This variable, y, is the size of an address. On most popular machines, an address is four bytes in size. Of course, this means that only one of x's four byte addresses will fit in the variable y. So, although y contains the address of a byte, that address will be used to refer to an integer, since we told the compiler that y contains an integer address.

If we look at this a bit more closely...

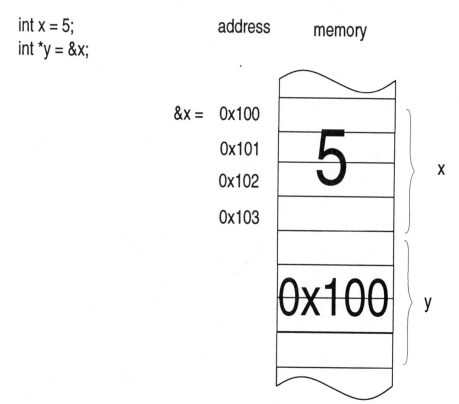

```
int x = 5;
int *y = &x;
```

A single address represents four addresses

Again, if you stop an think about this, it is not intuitive that the address of a byte would really point to a four byte integer: We are simply accustomed to the C compiler making assumptions "behind our back." Perhaps that is one of the reasons that new programmers find pointers difficult to understand. They are difficult to understand if no one explains that we should expect them to work in non-intuitive ways.

This brings up a concept which we will see in C++.

In C, we use the address of the lowest byte of an integer to represent the integer. We let the compiler work its "black magic" to use the whole integer even though we refer only to its first address.

In C++, we have a new type, called a "reference", which also behaves in non-intuituve ways. If behaves in non-intuitive ways simply because a variable was declared as a "reference." In some uses, a reference type acts like a pointer. In other uses, it acts in a completely different way. But I'm getting ahead of myself. We will be taking a closer look at references after we examine a few more C concepts that we need.

In C, there are other reasons that new programmers find pointers confusing. Since virtually every variable is at some address on the machine, there are two ways to access any variable. This leads to many errors during software development.

New programmers are often confused by addresses, since every memory location has a valid address.

It is easy to get lost in the profusion of address references and de-references.

A typical error would occur because the programmer takes the address of the wrong variable, and the compiler doesn't complain, since the programmer is allowed to use any address. This is the basic cause of the traditional "runaway pointer" problem which has plagued every C programmer.

For example, in a real program we might accidentally take the address of y, which is a valid address, but it might not be the value we are really trying to use.

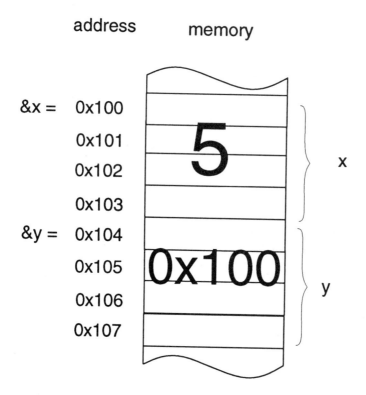

Too many things have valid addresses!

This also leads to memory problems: Not computer memory problems, but programmer's memory problems. That is, a programmer must remember whether he is currently working with the contents of a variable, or the address of a variable. This is hard to remember even in a small program: In a large program, it is impossible to remember, and it is often difficult to find the original declaration of a variable to determine its type.

C Problem

It is hard to remember whether any given variable is or isn't a pointer.

This leads to many programming errors.

As you probably guessed, I brought up this problem for a reason. The solution to this problem is found in C++

C++ Solution

Create a new variable type. It will act like a pointer only when you want it to.

Let the compiler figure out whether the variable should be accessed as a pointer based on the context in which the variable is used.

So, now we have the basic background to take a closer look at a new variable type, called a "reference" type. It can be similar to a pointer, and it can also be very different.

The Reference Type in C++

A reference type will sometimes act like a pointer to a variable, and sometimes act like the contents of the variable. The compiler decides which value you want.

Like classes in our last chapter, we need some way to declare this new type of variable. Like classes, we will steal ideas from existing practice in C.

In C, a definition of the form:

```
int x;
```

allocates space for an integer type.

A definition of the form

```
int *y;
```

allocates space for a pointer to an integer. That is, the "int *" is viewed by the compiler as defining a variable which holds an address of an integer.

We will use a new declaration which has the form such as:

```
int &x = 5;
```

That is, the "int &" declares a reference type. In this case, the integer is initialized to the value five.

Later, when you use the variable x, the compiler will sometimes use the address of the integer, and sometimes use the integer five itself

$$\text{int \& } \quad x = 5;$$

A new type --
Not just an integer
Not just the address of an integer

A "reference" type

The symbol "&" is not the address operator. That is because the address operator cannot be used in the definition of a variable. This statement has only one valid interpretation: And that is as a reference type in C++.

In C++ the address operator is still used in the same manner as in traditional C. The C++ language has simply *extended* the use of the operator symbol so that can have other meanings. In C, it would not have been possible to use the "&" symbol in a variable declaration. In C++, it can be used in a declaration, but it has a new interpretation: It declares a reference variable.

In the statement:

```
int &x = 5;
```

The compiler will determine whether the variable x refers to the value five, or the address of five. Your code will simply use the variable: The compiler will choose the correct interpretation.

(At least, that's the idea.)

Because a reference can access either the contents or the address of a variable, a reference must be initialized when it is declared. That is why I initialized my reference to five: I had to initialize it, otherwise the compiler would generate an error.

This dual nature of a single variable might be pictured this way:

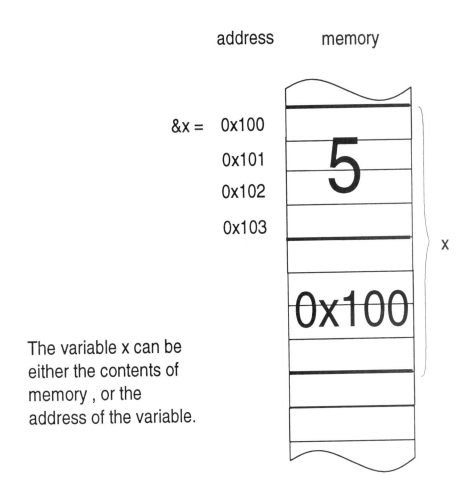

address   memory

&x =   0x100

0x101

0x102

0x103

x

The variable x can be
either the contents of
memory , or the
address of the variable.

One perspective on a reference type

In practice, there are some simple rules which let you know whether
the compiler will use an address or its contents.

In brief, any operator which acts on the variable will use the contents of the variable. This means:

```
int &  x = 5;
x=3;
```

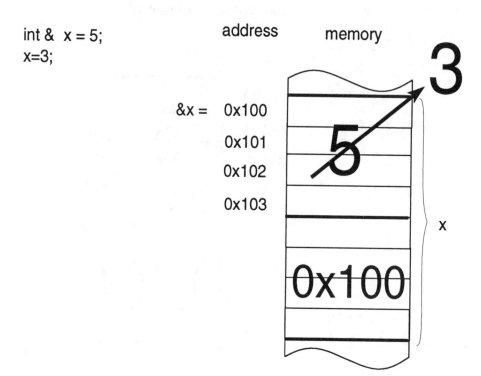

Operators act on the contents of the variable

So a statement such as

```
x = x+1;
```

will change the contents of x from five to six.

Anytime the variable is passed in a function call, the address will be passed. So a statement such as

```
myfunc(x);
```

Will cause the address of x to be passed on the stack to the receiving function.

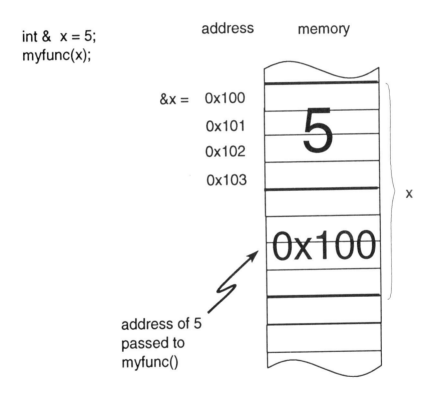

int & x = 5;
myfunc(x);

address   memory

&x =   0x100

        0x101   5
        0x102
        0x103   x

              0x100

address of 5
passed to
myfunc()

Function arguments use the variable's address

So the C++ reference type tries to act in an intuitive manner. It assumes that when you call a function, you will want to pass a pointer. .

Similarly, when an operator is used with a variable, it usually expects to operate on the contents of the variable. So, again, C++ tries to do the intuitive thing.

A Simple Example

This example should give you a better feel for the reference type. When you are examing this code, notice how the passed variable is declared in the receiving function.

```
refReceiver(int &var)
{
        var+=var;
}


receiver(int var)
{
        var+=var;
}


main()
{
        int y=2;

        printf("calling receiver...\n");
        receiver(y);
        printf("y=%x\n",y);

        printf("calling refReceiver...\n");
        refReceiver(y);
```

```
        printf("y=%x\n",y);
}
```

After putting this code into a file called "simple.c", it can be compiled using:

```
cc++ simple.c
```

When you run this code, you will notice that the function which is declared to receive a reference type gets passed the address of y. That means that the function which receives a reference modifies the same copy of the variable which the "main" routine uses.

On my machine, I invoke the program using the name "a.out"

```
$ a.out
calling receiver...
y=2
calling refReceiver...
y=4
```

The function which gets a simple integer receives a copy of the contents of y copied on to the stack: This is normal C operation. The variable which "main" uses is unmodified. The function modifies only the copy of the variable which is on the stack.

So, the compiler recognizes the reference type and does the right thing. A function which receives a reference type gets an address. A reference type which is passed to a function has its address passed.

References and Addresses

Although a reference type will automatically choose either the contents or the address, it is possible for the programmer to explicitly specify the address of a reference.

This is done in the usual C way: Using the address operator with the reference type.

```
main()
{
        int& ref=2;

        printf("ref=%x\n",ref);
        printf("&ref=%x\n",&ref);
}
```

Running this code yields

```
$ a.out
ref=2
&ref=3fffd00
```

Of course, the address of y will probably be different on your machine. Since y is a local variable, which is put on the stack, and will probably be in a different location on every machine.

The Simple Example: A closer look

Although the machine specifics vary, it is worthwhile to take a closer look at exactly what happens in our simple example. In particular, we will look at how the stack is used. Although this does not add any new information about references, it should help clarify their operation.

Of course, your machine may not do exactly the same things which are described here, but, in general, most machines do something very similar, if not exactly the same thing.

When the machine starts executing our simple example, it begins at the routine named `main()`, and continues sequentially. Stated another way, the machine's "program counter" register has the address for `main()`, which causes the machine to execute the instruction at that location.

The machine has also reserved some space for temporary storage. This storage, the "stack", is pointed to by the "stack pointer" register. This space is used to store any variables which are local to a function.

This diagram shows the "program counter" (pc) and the "stack pointer" (sp) registers of the machine. The `main()` function is about to begin executing, and the stack is empty.

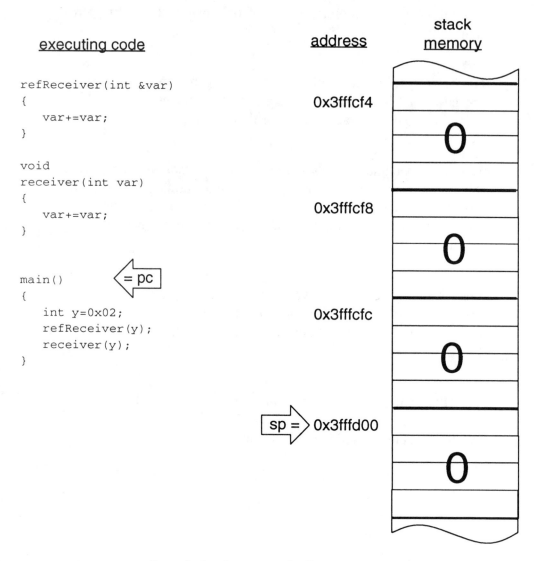

executing code   address   stack memory

```
refReceiver(int &var)
{
    var+=var;
}

void
receiver(int var)
{
    var+=var;
}

main()                         <= pc
{
    int y=0x02;
    refReceiver(y);
    receiver(y);
}
```

0x3fffcf4

0x3fffcf8

0x3fffcfc

sp => 0x3fffd00

Stack before main() executes

In the diagram, we see the stack pointer and addressess below it. That is because the stack grows downward in memory. That is, when a local variable is put on the stack, the "stack pointer" is decremented after the value is placed into stack memory.

When we execute the first line of our simple program, you will notice that our local variable y is placed on the stack, and the "stack pointer" has been decremented.

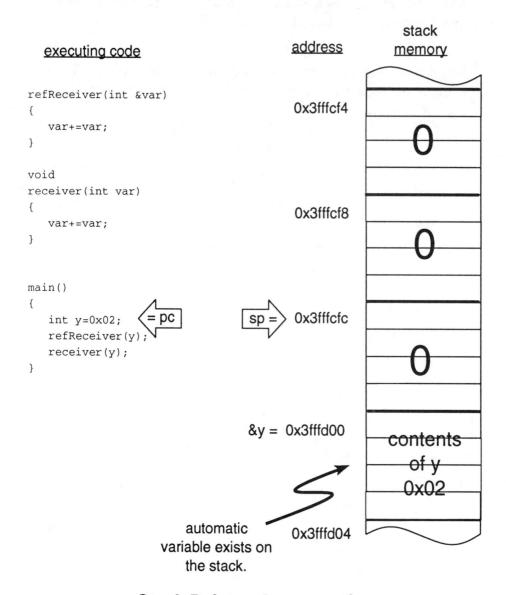

```
                                                 stack
    executing code               address        memory

refReceiver(int &var)
{                               0x3fffcf4
    var+=var;
}                                                  0

void
receiver(int var)
{                               0x3fffcf8
    var+=var;
}                                                  0

main()
{
    int y=0x02;   <= pc    sp => 0x3fffcfc
    refReceiver(y);
    receiver(y);                                   0
}

                    &y =  0x3fffd00           contents
                                                of y
                                                0x02

            automatic        0x3fffd04
        variable exists on
            the stack.
```

Stack Pointer decrementing

All arguments to functions are passed on the stack. That means that when the `refReceiver()` function is called, the argument y is copied on to the stack.

Since a function which expects to receive a reference is called, the stack looks like this:

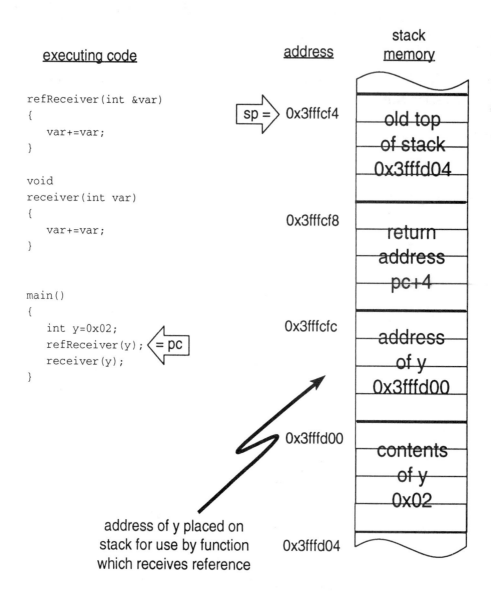

Calling a function expecting a reference

You will notice that the address of y was pushed on the stack by the compiler. The other thing which was pushed on the stack is the address where execution should continue when the function "refReceiver()" finishes executing, as well as the value for the old "top of stack."

So, when a function which expects a reference is invoked, the address of the argument is put on the stack. That means that the variable var in refReceiver() will get the address of y, allowing that function to modify the one copy of y which exists at 0x3fffd00.

This is in contrast to when receiver() is invoked. Since receiver() doesn't expect a reference argument, it gets a copy of y on the stack.

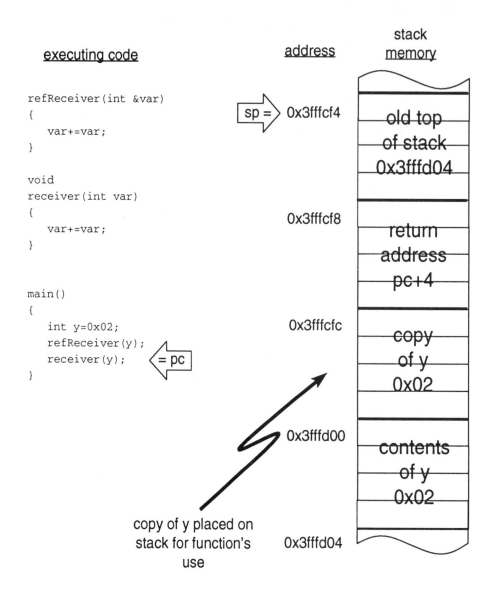

```
refReceiver(int &var)
{
    var+=var;
}

void
receiver(int var)
{
    var+=var;
}

main()
{
    int y=0x02;
    refReceiver(y);
    receiver(y);
}
```

executing code

address

stack memory

sp => 0x3fffcf4

old top
of stack
0x3fffd04

0x3fffcf8

return
address
pc+4

0x3fffcfc

copy
of y
0x02

0x3fffd00

contents
of y
0x02

= pc

copy of y placed on
stack for function's
use

0x3fffd04

Calling a typical function

Since `receiver()` does not use a reference argument, it gets a copy of the variable y. Any changes to the "var" variable in the function receiver() will only effect the copy of y at 0x3fffcfc, and not the original at 0x3fffd00.

The bottom line is that *you can't tell what is being pushed on the stack when you look at a function being invoked.* You *must* know how the function was defined.

Chapter Two

Chapter Three
Using Objects

In this Chapter we will take a closer look at objects and their use.

In particular, we will be examing some of the features which make objects useful for Object Oriented Programming. We have already seen their most important characteristic: They contain both data and code. That allows the "on demand" copying of code and data anytime in a program.

During this Chapter, we will be examining techniques for modifying the code and data which is in an object. This capability allows a "stock" object to be customized for a particular application. As we will see, there are several ways to modify the operation of an object.

What is an Object?

In the last chapter, we saw that an object is defined by a "class." The class definition describes which code and data should be included in an object.

We also saw that a class definition is very similar to a structure definition. In fact, there were only two major differences: the use of the keyword "public", and the fact that functions (ie. code) could be included in a class definition.

Structure	Class
| ```
struct myStructType {
    char x;
    int y;
    void *aptr;
}
``` | ```
class myClassType {
    char x;
    int y;
    void *aptr;
    int afunc(void);
}

myClassType::afunc(void)
{
    printf("in afunc\n");
}
``` |
| `struct myStructType st;` | `class myClassType cl;` |

Structures vs. Classes

The class shown above would cause the data, (x,y, and aptr) and code (afunc) to be placed in your program's address space, as the following diagram illustrates:

memory

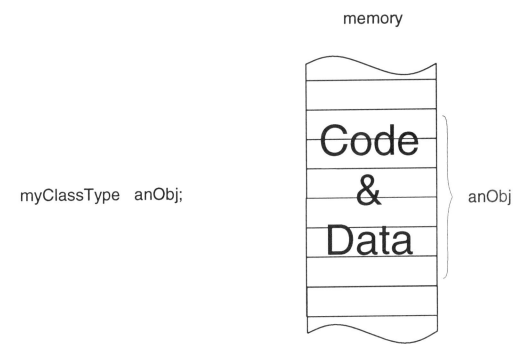

myClassType   anObj;

anObj

An Object contains code and data

So, an object has members which can be either code or data.

Although it is technically accurate to think of an object as code and data in memory, most of this chapter will use a simpler diagram to represent an object. That is because the emphasis is going to shift to the *interaction* of objects, rather than the specifics of a single object.

Classes with code in-line

It is possible to write the code for a function directly in the body of an object. We will create a simple object of class "classA" which has a single function, "afunc(void)."

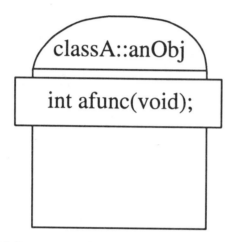

An Object can have a function in-line

Putting the code "in-line" with the class definition is an alternative to using the "::" operator to associate a function with a class, as the following code illustrates:

```
class classA {
   public:
         int x=5;
         int afunc(void)
         {
                 printf("in afunc of classA\n");
         }
};


   main()
```

```
{
        classA anObj;

        anObj.afunc();
}
```

When we put the code in the body of the class definition no external definition is necessary. This technique is typically used when the function body is only a few lines of code.

Using more than one Object

In this example, two objects are used.

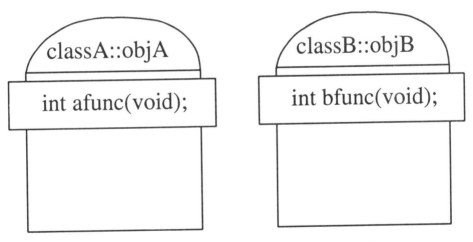

Multiple Objects can be used

This should seem intuitive to you at this point, but we are examining this just so that we are all clear about the use of objects. After all, they are the primary reason for learning C++.

```
class classA {
  public:
        int x=5;
        int afunc(void)
        {
                printf("in afunc of classA\n");
        }

};

class classB {
  public:
        int y=10;
        int bfunc(void)
        {
                printf("in bfunc of classB\n");
        }

};

main()
{
        classA objA;
        classB objB;

        printf("object A's x=%d\n",objA.x);
        printf("object B's y=%d\n",objB.y);
}
```

Running this program produces:

```
object A's x=5
object B's y=10
```

The function `main()` simply creates two objects: objA and objB. These objects are then each referenced individually.

It is important to be able to visualize objA and objB as distinct objects. It is obvious in this simple example, but it becomes less obvious when programs grow complex. I recommend that you picture both objA and objB as being dynamically allocated as automatic variables, each with its own code and data.

Multiple Objects of the same Class

In this example, we create several objects. Unlike the earlier examples, however, the objects are all of the same class. That means that they all have identically named variables and functions.

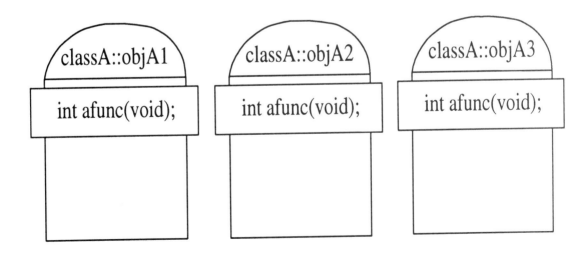

Remember: The objects themselves are distinct. They simply each have a variable named "x" and a function named "afunc."

```
class classA {
   public:
        int x=5;
        int afunc(void)
        {
            printf("in afunc of classA: x=%d\n",x++);
        }
};

main()
{
 classA  objA1, objA2, objA3;

 objA1.afunc();  /* prints & increments x of objA1 */
 objA2.afunc();  /* prints & increments x of objA2 */
 objA1.afunc();  /* prints & increments x of objA1 */
}
```

Running this program yields:

```
in afunc of classA: x=5
in afunc of classA: x=5
in afunc of classA: x=6
```

Now we are getting a first glimpse of the power of Object Oriented Programming. Since each object has essentially a well contained set of code and data, that object becomes a reusable piece of code which can be more easily integrated with another programmer's code.

That is because the variables and functions in objects have names which are distinct from names used outside an object. Our code above has three variables named x. The compiler automatically associates a variable with its object.

This is, however, just a hint of the power of C++.We will begin examining some ways to modify existing objects. This will allow us to take an existing object and customize it for our use.

Adding Code or Data

One of the ways which you can modify an object is by adding some new C code to an existing class.

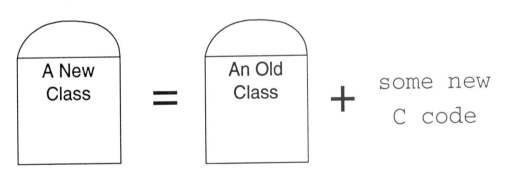

Classes can be extended

There is only one thing which we need to add to our existing knowledge about objects in order to add code. And that is just some simple syntax. It is possible specify that a class includes the code and data of another class using a ":". For example, the code:

```
class newClass: oldClass {
   public:
        int x;
   }
```

would specify that the "newClass" should inherit all the code and data from the class "oldClass." In addition, the new data item "x" is added to "newClass."

This is a very useful feature. A simple example of its use is:

```
class base {
        public:
                int x=5;
};

class derived: public base {
        public:
                int y=10;
};

main()
{
  derived objD;

  printf("objD has both objects: x=%d y=%d\n",
        objD.x, objD.y);
}
```

Running this code gives us:

```
objD has both objects: x=5 y=10
```

You probably noticed the keyword "`public`" in the above example. That is because C++ will, by default, consider the elements of `base` inaccessable to `derived` unless the keyword "`public`" is used. Again, where traditional C was open and unforgiving, C++ is restrictive and more forgiving: since the compiler is able to catch inadvertent accesses.

Vocabulary Excursion

We've already examined a number of new concepts: Now we will take the time to associate the "lingo" with the ideas we've been examining.

In the last example, we had an "old class" which was modified to create a "new class." In C++, the "old class" is considered the "base class".

And, the "new class" is called the "derived class." It is derived from the base class.

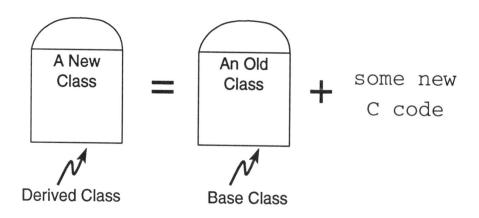

Base and Derived Classes

In general, a class which "provides" code is called a base class, and a class which "receives" code from another class is called a derived class.

And, although we have pictured the modification of an object as addition, the correct terminology is "inheritance."

An object which shares code with another object is said to "inherit" from the base object. Pictorially, a derived class is shown with an arrow pointing to its base class: That is because the derived class is a superset of the code of the base class.

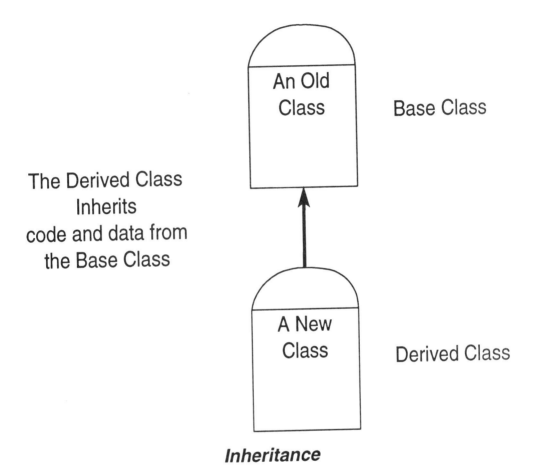

The Derived Class
Inherits
code and data from
the Base Class

Base Class

Derived Class

Inheritance

When functions are in objects, I've sometimes referred to those functions as "member" functions of the objects. That is, in fact, correct terminology for C++. In addition, the more general term used in Object Oriented Programming can be applied: That is, functions which are in objects can be called "methods."

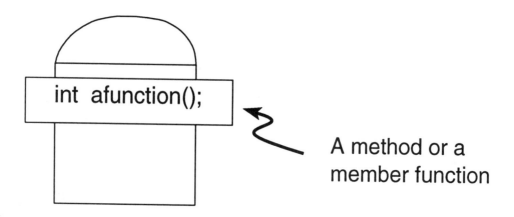

Functions in Objects are methods

There is another term which is commonly used in Object Oriented Programming, but is not so commonly used in C++: That is referring to function(method) invocation as "messaging."

On occasion, articles on C++ will refer to sending a message, but it is more common to hear it called either a "function call" or "method invocation."

Replacing Code or Data: Overriding

In the previous example, we *added* some data. This time we will *replace* some data in an existing object. The idea is:

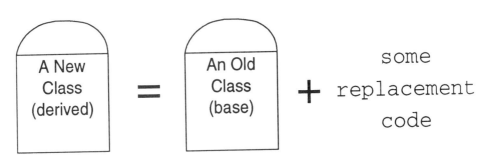

Classes can be modified

A simple example of this, in which we replace the variable x, would be:

```
class Base {
        public:
                int x=5;
};

class Derived: public Base {
        public:
                int x=10;
};

main()
{
        Derived objD;

        printf("objD has both objects: x=%d\n",
            objD.x);
}
```

Running this code produces:

```
objD has both objects: x=10
```

So replacing code is as simple as using a variable with the same name. Of course, if the architect of the original object did not want you to be able to "override" a variable, he would not have made it a public variable in the original(base) object.

We will be taking a closer look at alternatives to "public" access in Chapter Six.

Replacing Code: A much better way

We've seen that it is possible to override a variable or function. We simply create a variable or function of the same name in our new object.

But it is much better to *design* an object so that some functions can be implemented by another object. In fact, many people consider such design to be the essence of Object Oriented Programming (OOP).

The problem with overriding is that the original(base) object *did not know* which functions were going to be overridden. That means that those functions may do operations which are necessary to the correct function of the object. If those functions are overriden, the object may stop working.

If, on the other hand, an object is designed so that certain functions can be implemented by another object, then it is possible to safely replace code and data in the derived object. This provides a "clean" way of organizing code.

We will look at another small piece of code which replaces code in an original class. This code will illustrate the "better way" to replace code in a class.

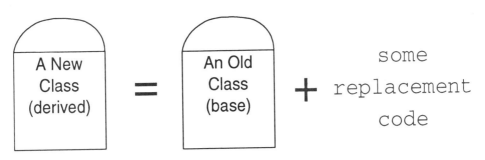

Classes can be modified by Design

If a function will be implemented by another class, it is designated as "virtual" in C++.

The "virtual" keyword tells the class that a derived class should have the code which actually implements the function.

A simple example of this, in which we replace the function `Base-func()`, would be:

```
class Base {
        public:
```

```
                int x;
                 virtual int Basefunc(void)
                 {
                 printf("in Basefunc\n");
                 }


};

class Derived: public Base {
        public:
                int y;
                 int Basefunc(void)
                 {
                 printf("in Derived version of
Basefunc\n");
                 }
};

main()
{
        Base objB;
        Derived objD;

        objB.Basefunc();
        objD.Basefunc();
}
```

When we run this code, the output looks like:

```
in Basefunc
in Derived version of Basefunc
```

It may, at first, appear that the keyword virtual is nothing more than a comment. But that is not true.

The keyword virtual means that `Base` will keep a *pointer* to the implementation of the virtual function. So class `Base` will know two implementations for the function `Basefunc()`. It will know its own implementation, and it will have a pointer to a future implementation, which will be initialized by a derived object.

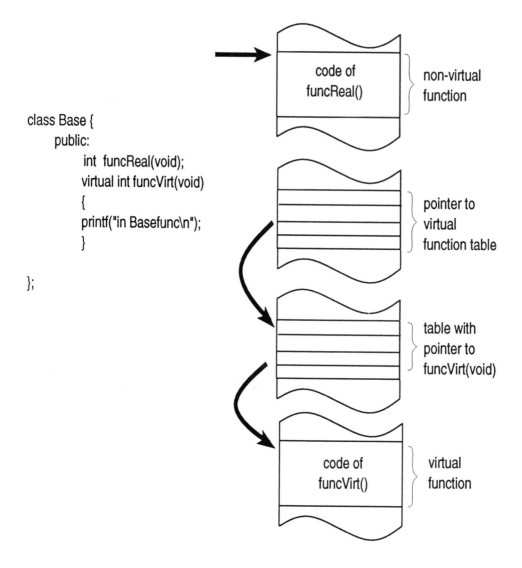

```
class Base {
    public:
        int  funcReal(void);
        virtual int funcVirt(void)
        {
        printf("in Basefunc\n");
        }

};
```

Virtual Function in Memory

This begs the question: If Base has two implementations of Base-func(), how do we know which implementation we are accessing?

The answer is: If a derived class implements a virtual function, it never invokes the base class implementaion.

That is because the keyword virtual tells the compiler to initialize the pointer to the new implementation. The pointer is set when the derived class is created.

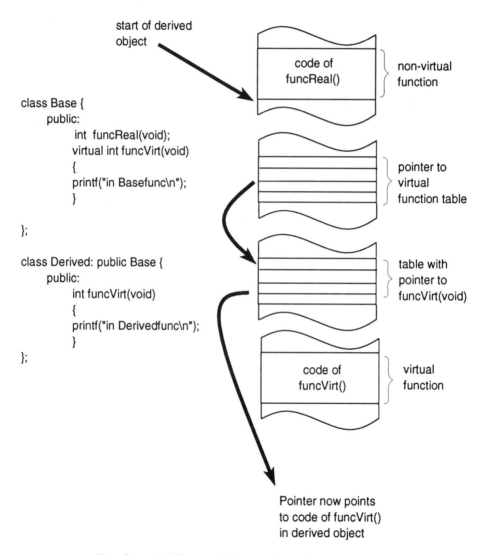

start of derived
object

code of
funcReal()

} non-virtual
function

```
class Base {
    public:
        int  funcReal(void);
        virtual int funcVirt(void)
        {
        printf("in Basefunc\n");
        }

};
```

} pointer to
virtual
function table

```
class Derived: public Base {
    public:
        int funcVirt(void)
        {
        printf("in Derivedfunc\n");
        }
};
```

} table with
pointer to
funcVirt(void)

code of
funcVirt()

} virtual
function

Pointer now points
to code of funcVirt()
in derived object

Derived Virtual Function in Memory

The use of the keyword virtual is important. It is worth studying this
next example closely. It illustrates that a derived class uses the function from the derived class, *even if we tell the compiler that it is the*

base class!

```
class Base {
        public:
                int x;
                 virtual int Basefunc(void)
                 {
                 printf("in Basefunc\n");
                 }

};

class Derived: public Base {
        public:
                int y;
                 int Basefunc(void)
                 {
                 printf("in Derived Basefunc\n");
                 }
};

main()
{
        Base objB;
        Derived objD;

        Base *basePointer=&objD; // addr of objD

        objB.Basefunc();
        objD.Basefunc();
        basePointer->Basefunc();
}
```

Running this code produced:

```
in Basefunc
in Derived Basefunc
in Derived Basefunc
```

There are two important points in this section.

1) Use the keyword virtual to indicate that a function will be implemented in a derived class.

2) Each object has, embedded in the object itself, pointers to its functions. That means that we can tell the compiler that the object is of a different class, but the object itself will still have internal pointers appropriate to its class.

Virtual Functions == OOP??

There are some subtle implications for Object Oriented Programming in the last example.

You may not have noticed it, but we were able to tell a derived object that it was really a base object. (That is, we told the compiler to modify the address of the derived object so that it pointed to the base portions of the object. That is what the cast does: It adds an offset to the address before using it.)

Just to make the significance a bit more concrete, imagine that you are programming an application which puts holes into surfaces using a machine. You might have objects representing holes, and objects representing surfaces.

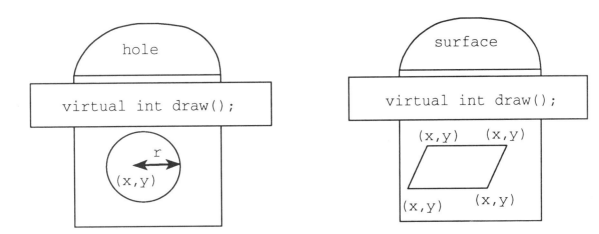

Objects with code and data

You probably have other functions which operate on either holes or surfaces. That is, you might have a library function which looks like:

```
int putHoleInSurface(hole& h, surface& s);
```

Of course, this function expects to operate on objects of your type, ie. holes and surfaces. Further, this function may call draw() in each of the objects after doing appropriate data manipulation.

The draw functions are virtual, since you want to allow the interactive portion of your program to be adapted to different computers: One computer may use PostScript, another may use PHIGS. As is often the case, another programmer may do the interface for a different machine.

You give your code to someone who does the user interface. That programmer then creates new objects, derived from your objects. He then implements the `draw()` function in both the hole and surface objects. *But he is still able to call your function, putHoleInSurface(), which expects objects of your base types.*

But that is not all. The original functions you created will work, and will be able to call the functions provided by the new programmer, his `draw()` functions, as long as they were designated as virtual functions in your base classes. (Since the objects themselves store the pointers. If your function gets an object which is the base type, it will get the function from the base class. If it gets a derived object, a pointer *in the object* will have been modified, and the virtual function will be called instead.)

Objects: A matter of Life and Death

In C++, the initialization sequence is somewhat different than in ANSI C. In the typical C program, there are several modules linked together, starting with a module called "crt0.o", which is the initialization module for C. This module will typically do any initialization which may be necessary for the Operating System or Shared Libraries, and then call your `main()` function.

In C++, there is typically another module which is called before your `main()` function. It initializes any objects which you have statically declared. For example:

```
class myClassType {
   int x;
}

static class myClassType anObject;

main()
{
/* do whatever here */
}
```

This code does not dynamically create the object "anObject." Instead, it is statically declared. That means that it must be allocated and initialized before your code begins to execute. The initialization is done before the main() routine is called.

In addition, it is possible for the programmer to specify a routine which is to be called when an object is initialized. As you might expect, it is also possible to specify a routine which is invoked when an object is destroyed.

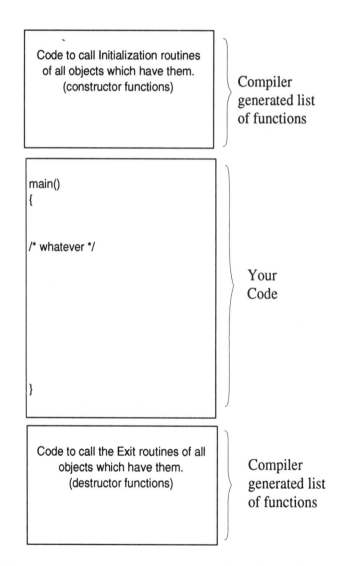

C++ generates startup and exit code

A routine which initializes an object is called a "constructor." A routine which is called at the end of your object's life is called a "destructor." We will look at both in more detail.

Initializing Your Object

By default, the C++ compiler will assume that a function having the same name as the class will be the constructor. For example:

```
class classA {
        public:
                int x=5;
        classA(void)
        {
                printf("in constructor\n");
        }
};



main()
{
        classA objA;
        /* ... */
}
```

Destroying Your Object

The code which invokes your `main()` routine will also be called when your `main()` routine exits. That means that it is able to call and "destructor" routines which you may have specified for your objects. Like constructors, there is a default routine which is invoked.

It will have the same name as you class, with a tilde added in front of the name.

```
class classA {
        public:
                int x=5;
        ~classA(void)
        {
                printf("in destructor\n");
        }
};
```

So, putting it all together, it is possible to create an object which has routines which are automatically called when the object is created and when it is destroyed.

```
class classA {
        public:
                int x=5;
        classA(void)
        {
                printf("in constructor\n");
        }
        ~classA()
        {
                printf("in destructor\n");
        }
};


main()
{
```

```
        classA objA;

        sleep(2);
    }
```

Running this produces:

```
    in constructor
    in destructor
```

The sequence in which constructors are called is not guaranteed: That means that you cannot assume that another object is initialized when you use a constructor. Obviously, this can be a severe limitation for the use of constructors: It forces programmers to create code in each object which initializes a variable, so that the variable can be tested to find out if the object has started execution.

Self References

It is not unusual to to have an object which calls another function in *the same* object. In this next example, we will see a function called afunc() which wants to invoke bfunc() in the same object.

```
    class classA {
        public:
            int x;
            int afunc(void)
              {
              printf("in afunc of classA\n");
              /* now call bfunc. But how?? */
              }
```

```
        int bfunc(void)
          {
          printf("in bfunc of classA\n");
          }
  };
```

This may, at first glance, appear simple, but it is not.

The problem is that there may be many copies of bfunc(), since there may be many objects of type classA. For example:

```
  main()
  {
      classA objA1, objA2;

      objA1.afunc();
  }
```

This would create objects objA1 and objA2.

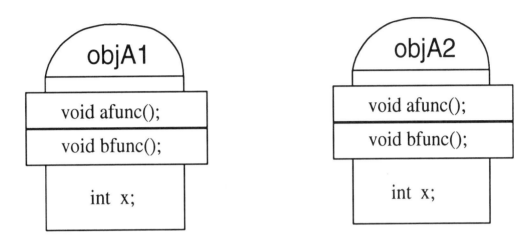

In order for an object to call another function within it, that object must have a pointer to itself.

Fortunately, C++ provides a variable which is guaranteed, on entry to an object's function, to be initialized to be a pointer to the current object. The variable is called "this."

So, rewriting the above code to use the "this" pointer,

```
class classA {
    public:
        int x;
        int afunc(void)
          {
            printf("in afunc of classA\n");
            this->bfunc();
```

```
            }
        int bfunc(void)
            {
            printf("in bfunc of classA\n");
            }
    };
    main()
    {
        classA objA1, objA2;

        objA1.afunc();
    }
```

Running this produces:

```
in afunc of classA
in bfunc of classA
```

Practically speaking, the "this" pointer is passed to each member function as an argument on the stack. That is, there is a hidden argument to all functions in objects: That hidden argument is the "this" pointer. Although C++ simply guarantees that the "this" pointer will exist, all current C++ implementations use the "hidden argument" method to initialize "this" for each function.

Chapter Four
Function Name Reuse

In this Chapter we will be taking a closer look at at how C++ handles function and operator names. This is especially significant because the concept of a "function pointer" is no longer the same as in ANSI C.

Also, we will discover that C++ often changes the names of functions which we define:Surprisingly, we must understand how the compiler "manipulates" the names in order to debug code in a reasonable amount of time.

Name Reuse

We've already seen that it is possible to have functions of the same name in two different classes: This is analagous to structures, which can have members of the same name, as long as they are in different structures.

If, for example, we have code such as

```
class classA {
   int afunc(void);
```

```
    }

    class classB {
        int afunc(void);
    }
```

There is no name confict. Since we've created distinct classes.

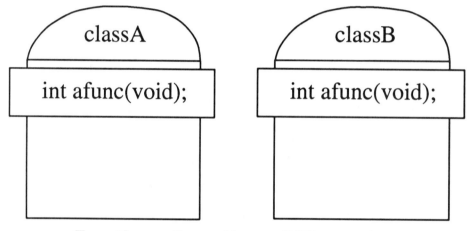

Functions: Same Name, Different Classes

In C++ terminology, we can refer to the functions as:

```
    classA::afunc(void)
```

or

```
    classB::afunc(void);
```

But this is just the first hint of name reuse. Not only can the same name be used in different classes: The same name can be reused in the same class! This is called "function overloading."

Overloading Member Functions

We can have as many versions of `afunc()` as we want, as long as we adhere to one restriction: Each version of `afunc()` must take different arguments. For example:

```
class classA{
   int afunc(void);
   int afunc(int);
}
```

This would create an object which has two distinct functions:

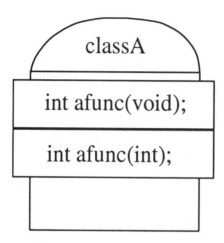

Same Name, Same Class (Args differ)

Although this is a nice feature, the ability to keep function names distinct may seem puzzling: And it should seem puzzling!

The natural question to ask is "How can the loader distinguish the names?" And the answer is: *C++ selects a name for your function!*

That is, the C++ compiler will look at the arguments which your function takes, and choose an arbitrary name so that the loader can resolve references to that function.

For example, the loader might map names using an encoding of the class name and the argument type:

```
classA {
     public:
     int  afunc(int)
     {
              /* ... */
     };
     int  afunc(void)
     {
              /* ... */
     };
};
```

_afunc__6classAi
to the compiler and
loader

_afunc__6classA
to the compiler
and loader

C++ internally maps function names

An example of this "remapping" in action is:

```
class classA {
        public:
                int afunc(int x)
                { printf("in afunc with int arg\n"); }
                int afunc(void)
                { printf("in afunc with void arg\n"); }
        };
```

```
main()
{
        classA objA;
        objA.afunc((int)10);
        objA.afunc();
}
```

When run, the program produces the following output:

```
in afunc with int arg
in afunc with void arg
```

We can see how the C++ compiler renames the functions if we intentionally give unresolved references to the compiler. I tried to compile the following code, which does not define the member functions.

```
class classA {
        public:
                int afunc(int x);
                int afunc(void);
};
```

```
main()
{
        classA objA;
        objA.afunc((int)10);
```

```
        objA.afunc();
}
```

My compiler (GNU 1.37 with NeXT modifications) displays the following when I try to compile and link the code:

```
cc++  -g -I/C++/Libg++-1.37.0 -I/C++/Libg++-1.37.0/
g++-include  test.c -lg++
/bin/ld: Undefined symbols:
_afunc__6classA
_afunc__6classAi
*** Exit 1
Stop.
```

So, although C++ hides the mapping, we must be aware of the mapping conventions in order to figure out the loader's error messages.

Unfortunately, the C++ mapping of function names is implementation dependent. Figuring out how your compiler maps names is usually a matter of trial and error.

In this section, we have been looking at functions which are in classes. But, in general, the same encoding applies to functions outside of objects ("global" functions)

Overloading Global Functions

It is also possible to reuse the name of "normal" C functions.

The only difference is this: When we overload functions outside of an object, we use the keyword "overload" to tell the compiler that we intend to overload the function.

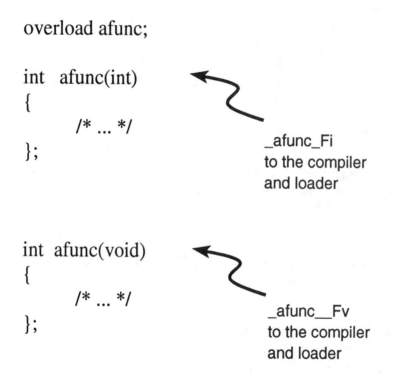

```
overload afunc;

int  afunc(int)
{
        /* ... */
};
```

_afunc_Fi
to the compiler
and loader

```
int  afunc(void)
{
        /* ... */
};
```

_afunc__Fv
to the compiler
and loader

Use "overload" for non-member functions

An example of this would be:

```
overload afunc;

int afunc(int x)
{
   printf("in global afunc with int arg\n");
}

int afunc(void)
{
   printf("in global afunc with void arg\n");
}

main()
{
   afunc((int)10);
   afunc();
}
```

Compiling and running this code yields:

```
in global afunc with int arg
in global afunc with void arg
```

An Important Detail: Function Arguments

It might seem useful to have the arguments encoded in the function name: And, in fact, it is. But don't assume that the argument list which C++ generates, or the argument list which you specify for the function, is correct.

In fact, all current C++ compilers pass an additional, "hidden" argument to all functions which are members of objects. The additional argument is the "this" pointer which points to the current object.

```
classA {
      public:
      int  afunc(int)
      {
      /* ... */
      };
      int  afunc(void)
      {
      /* ... */
      };
};

afunc(classA *, int)
```

The "this" hidden
argument

C++ passes hidden arguments

The fact that C++ does this is quite significant. Unlike C, you can never be sure of what C++ is passing to your functions.

Also, you are no longer able to use a function pointer to invoke a function: You no longer know what arguments to pass to the function. Any given implementation of C++ may or may not pass the `this` pointer on the stack.

Also, the compiler must be informed of the type of pointer. A pointer to a member function must know which object it points to, otherwise the C++ compiler cannot put the correct argument on the stack.

Also, function pointers are no longer equivalent. A pointer to a "global" function cannot be used as a pointer to a member function, and vice versa. That is because the compiler must decide what gets passed to the function.

The restrictions on function pointers goes beyond arguments which are being passed. If a derived object is cast to a base object, the compiler calculates a new address for the this pointer, as well as using an address based on the type of object which is being cast to. In other words, the compiler is responsible for manipulating all addresses associated with an object.

We will be taking a closer look at pointer's in the "Objects Revisited" chapter.

Another Type of Overloading

We are all accostomed to a typical function call, something of the form:

```
main(int argc, char *argv)
{
   afunc();/* call afunc */
}
```

But there is another way to invoke functions: A way we, as C programmers, are not accustomed to.

It is possible to have any of the following *operators* invoke any function you select:

+   -   *   /   %   ^   & | ~

!   =   <   >   +=   -=   *=

/=   %=   ^=   &= |=   <<

>>   >>=   <<=   ==   !=   <=

>=   && || ++   --   []   ()

new   delete

Can be redefined to call a function

This is called "operator overloading," and it allows a statement to invoke a function. For example, "overloading" the "+" symbol would allow:

```
objC = objA + objB;        /* invoke "+" function */
```

This would permit any function you specify to "add" the objects objA and objB.

Creating this functionality is as simple as defining a function to be invoked when the "+" symbol is encountered. The syntax for the function definition is slighly unusual, however.

103

The function is given a name which has the word "operator" attached to the operator symbol itself. We might think of the syntax as:

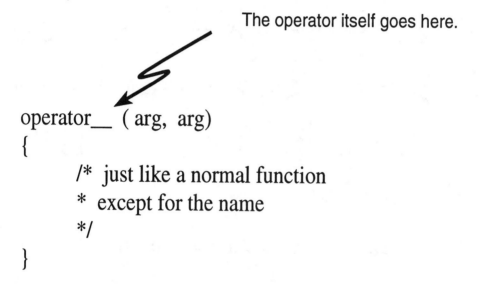

The operator itself goes here.

```
operator__ ( arg,  arg)
{
      /*  just like a normal function
      *  except for the name
      */
}
```

Redefining Operators

An example of overloading the "+" operator to multiply is:

```
class classA
{
   public:
       int x=2;
};

class classB
```

```
{
   public:
      int y=3;
};

int operator+(classA& objA, classB& objB)
{
   printf("in + operator: multiplying!\n");
   return (objA.x * objB.y);
}

main()
{
   classA objA;
   classB objB;
   int result;

   result = objA + objB;
   printf("result=%d\n",result);
}
```

Running this program produces:

```
in + operator: multiplying!
result=6
```

While this might seem odd, operator overloading can improve program readability. The classic example involves vectors, which have vector addition, vector subtraction, and vector multiplication associated with them. With the help of the C++ compiler, a vector object would be able to use the same operators that we are accustomed to.

There are some significant constraints to operator overloading, however. In particular, operator overloading must involve objects. There are two rules enforced by the compiler:

1) An argument to the overloaded operator must be an object

or

2) The overloading must be an object method

Also, the operator keeps many of its original characteristics. If we are using an operator that expects two operands normally, it can only be made to use two operands.

Similarly, the precedence rules still apply to the operator.

These restrictions make sense if we remember that C++ was designed to extend the C+ language, rather than to change it.

Chapter Five
Objects Revisited

This Chapter is a collection of topics.

But, unlike the "Miscellaneous Features" Chapter, the topics in this Chapter are just too important to push to the end of the book.

We will start by reviewing how objects are created, in order to take a closer look at the scope of objects. This will also be a lead-in to the the techniques of dynamic object creation.

Since pointers to functions are used in dynamic object creation, we will then look at pointers to functions and pointers to member functions. Unfortunately, these are two different types of pointers.

Finally, we will finish up with a closer look at inheritance. This will be a quick introduction to the potentially compex topics which inheritance can generate. Many simple relationships can become very obscure as the number and types of objects increase.

Where is an object known?

In traditional C, it often takes years to appreciate the meaning of "extern," "static," and "automatic." C++ takes those and builds upon them.

We are all familiar with a typical C function. In general, C functions have file scope: Which is another way of saying that the function name is recognized anywhere in the file.

File

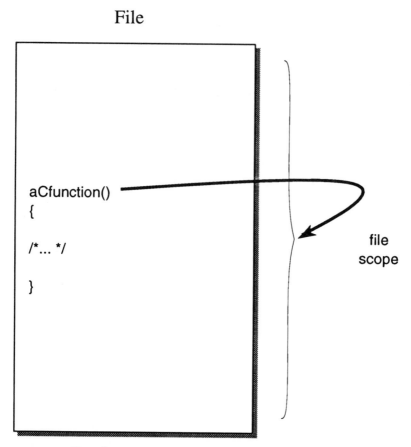

Typical C function with file scope

The scope of member functions is not so straightforward, however.

File

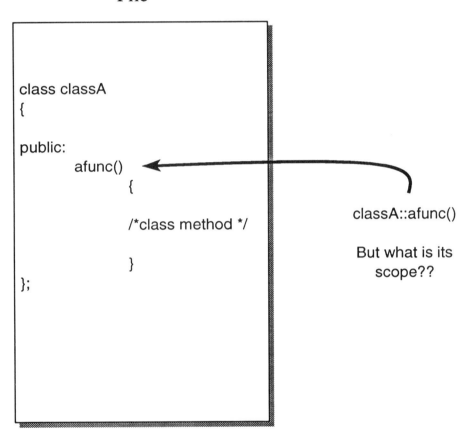

Scope depends on Object

The problem is that objects themselves have a scope associated with them. And the scope of their functions is limited to the scope of the object which contains it.

There are two possible types of object: static and automatic.

A static object has file scope, while an automatic object has block scope.

File

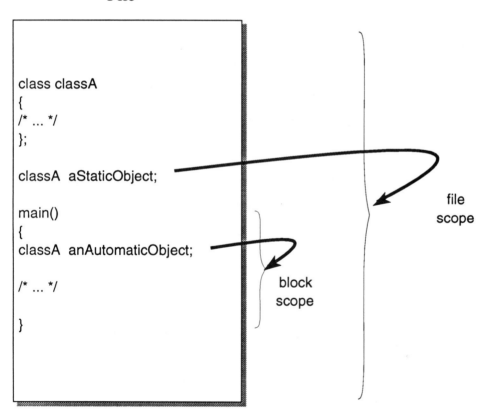

```
class classA
{
/* ... */
};

classA  aStaticObject;

main()
{
classA  anAutomaticObject;

/* ... */

}
```

block
scope

file
scope

Static and Automatic Scope

In an earlier chapter we saw that classes can also have constructors and destructors associated with them.

The scope of the object determines when those functions are invoked.

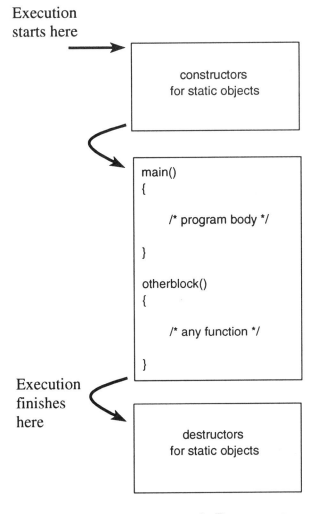

Static Object Constructos & Destructors

This is in contrast to an automatic object, which has its constructors invoked at the start of the block which contains it; and its destructors invoked at the end of the block.

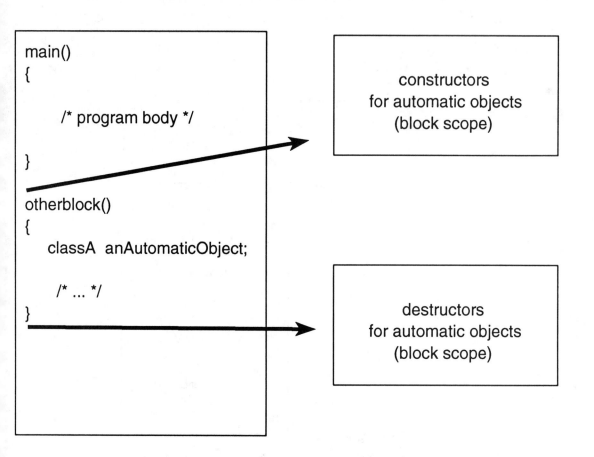

The block determines when initialized

Dynamic Object Creation

It is also possible to create objects "on the fly." Of course, this is useful in many situations, such as interactive programs which create data structures based on user input. Dynamic allocation of space has always been a major shortcoming of ANSI C, which relies on "malloc", "calloc", and "realloc."

The dynamic creation of an object is straightforward, with the use of the "new" operator, which will return a pointer to an object. A simple example is:

```
class classA
{
   int afunc(){printf("in afunc\n");}
};

main()
{
   classA *ptr;
   ptr = new classA;
}
```

An object created this way will have file scope.

File

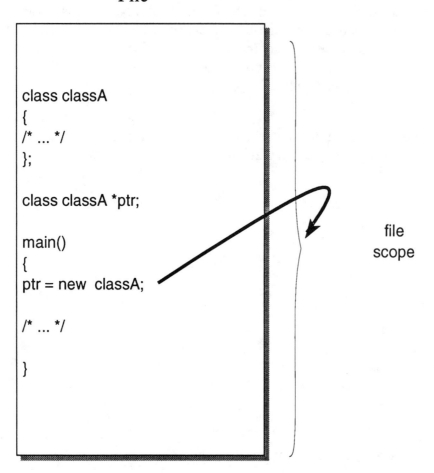

```
class classA
{
/* ... */
};

class classA *ptr;

main()
{
ptr = new  classA;

/* ... */

}
```

file
scope

Dynamic Objects have file scope

Objects which are created with new can only be deallocated with the operator "delete." It is not possible to use any of the other ANSI C mechanisms to free space.

An example of the use of delete is:

File

```
class classA
{
/* ... */
};

class classA *ptr;

main()
{
ptr = new  classA;

/* ... */

delete ptr;

}
```

delete objects created with new

On any machine, even with virtual address architectures, there is a limit to the amount of space which can be allocated. In C++, the "new" operator is designed to call a function when it cannot allocate sufficient space for the new data structure.

This error handling function has a well defined name, but no address associated with it.

Of course, every C function must have an address.

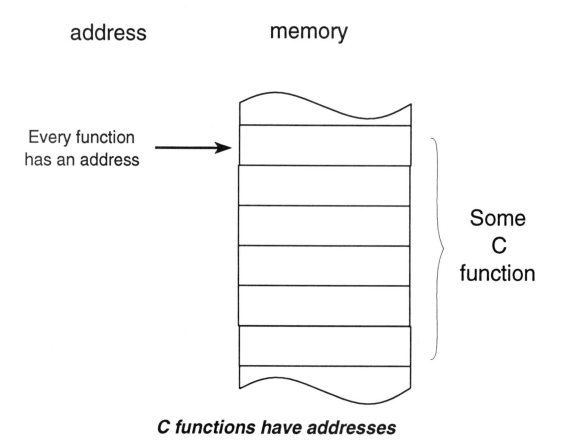

C functions have addresses

The typical technique used to asssign an address to a function involves setting a name to an address. A version which works for a typical C function in C++ is:

address   memory

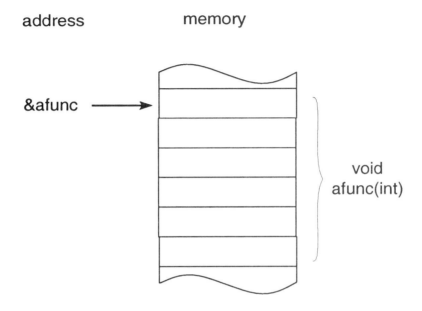

declaration: typedef void (*P)(int);
assignment: P ptr = &afunc;
invocation: (*ptr)(5);

This same code works in C, but most programmers do not go through so much effort to specify the type. Of course, since C++ depends on the type in order to "adjust addresses" and check types, this type of declaration is required in C++.

In the case of the C++ error handling function for the "new" operator, it is named "_new_handler", and can be set using a technique like the one shown above.

Although this pointer can be set in the typical manner, it is not very useful in practice. Most modern machines allow the allocation of virtual storage, and only fail when that virtual storage is referenced, and there is no more physical storage (ie disk swap space) which can be allocated.

In C programs, the ability to set function addresses is often used in jump tables and in programs which access PROMs or use some other Operating System routine which is located at a known memory address. So the ability of C++ to use function pointers is important.

But, as we will see, there are some differences between these pointers.

Pointers to Member Functions

Although, as we have just seen, function pointers are unchanged from ANSI C, that is not true for member functions.

The technique for using pointers to member functions is similar to that used by C. The major difference is the requirement for the explicit declaration of the type of the function.

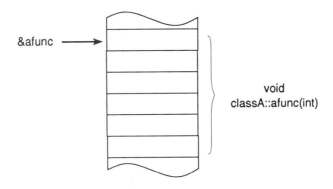

```
declaration:  void (classA::*P)(int);
assignment:  P  ptr = &classA::afunc;
invocation:  (obj.*ptr)(5);
```

Pointers to Member Function

An example of the use is:

```
class classA
{
   public:
   void afunc(int x) { printf("x = %d\n",x); };
};

typedef void (classA::*P)(int);

main()
{
   classA objA;
   P ptr=&classA::afunc;

   (objA.*ptr)(5);
```

}

Other Types of Inheritance

So far in this book, we have always seen objects which inherit from a single object. In an earlier chapter we discussed the possibility of having a hole and a surface object, each of which allow new objects to be derived.

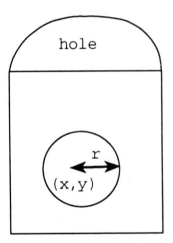

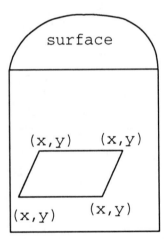

Hole and Surface Objects

It is easy to imagine a scenario where we might want a new object which always has a hole. This might be called a "plate" object, and we would want it to be derived from *both* a hole and a surface.

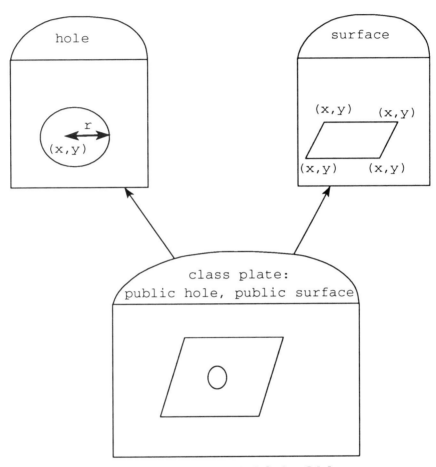

Inheritance from Multiple Objects

Some code which illustrates multiple inheritance is:

```
class hole {
    public:
        int radius=8;
        int xcenter=50,ycenter=50;
```

```
    };

    class surface{
        public:
            int x[4],y[4];         // four corners
    };

    class plate: public hole, public surface
    {
        int side=1;                // top plate by default
    };

    main()
    {
        plate objP;
        /* ... */
    }
```

This is fairly straightforward so far. This is a simple extension of the inheritance we have seen in earlier chapters.

But image that we want to have a display window associated with these objects.

And imagine that we want to create an object which knows how to initialize that display window.

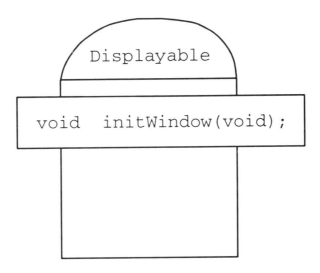

An object to initialize a Window

And, we decide that we want both hole and surface to be derived from this object.

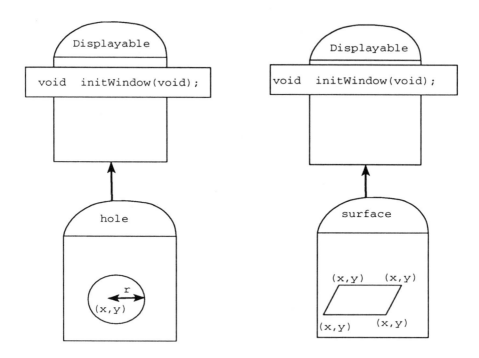

Both hole and surface are "displayable"

Suddenly, our plate object has gotten very complicated. That is because it now has *two* copies of the initWindow routine.

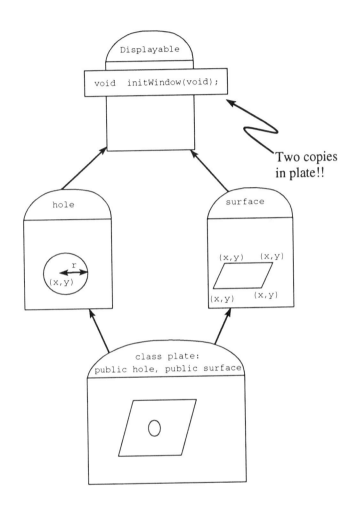

Multiple Inheritance complication

Of course, there is a solution to this problem.

C++ allows a class to indicate that only one copy of its routines should exist in any derived object. This is done with the keyword "virtual." An example is:

```
virtual class displayable {
   public:
        initWindow(){printf("in initWindow\n");};
};

class hole: public displayable {
   public:
        int radius=8;
        int xcenter=50,ycenter=50;
};

class surface: public displayable {
   public:
        int x[4],y[4];          // four corners
};

class plate: public hole, public surface {
     int side=1;               // top plate by default
};

main()
{
   plate objP;
   /* ... */
}
```

Although not specific to multiple inheritance, just as a function may be copied multiple times, a variable may be copied multiple times.

This can be avoided by declaring the variable "static."

For example, we might have a variable which keeps track of all holes in a surface. This might be defined as a static array:

```
static hole *holeList[10];    // holes in surface
```

Our modified surface object might look like:

```
class surface: public displayable {
   public:
    int x[4],y[4];         // four corners
    static hole *holeList[10]; // holes in surface
};
```

Defining it in this way ensures that only one copy will exist.

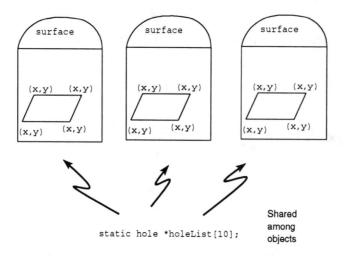

static hole *holeList[10];

Shared among objects

Static variable are shared

We have really only "scratched the surface" in terms of what can happen in inheritance.

And, not all inheritance problems have solutions which are straight-forward, or even understandable.

And, even if the issue is addressed by the language, there is always the question of whether the compiler writer interpreted the specification in the same way.

Chapter Six
Enforcing Object Integrity

For the most part, we have been ignoring the issues of data sharing between objects. But, like real life, sooner or later we must address such issues.

Fortunately, there are C++ keywords which allow us to restrict access to the functions(methods) and data contained in an object.

Unfortunately, there can be some subtle interactions between those keywords when inheritance is involved: In fact, for some complicated cases, trial and error is far easier than trying to understand which rules are involved for your particular hierarchy of objects.

In this chapter, we will be examining the common cases of restricting object access.

Object Security

In every class we've defined so far, we've gone out of our way to make sure that all elements are public, which allows anyone to access them

```
class Base {
   public:
         /* ... */
};
```

Similarly, when we've used inheritance, we've always made sure that we specified the base class as public to our new class:

```
class Derived: public Base {
   /* ... */
};
```

We've done this because anyone can invoke a function which is public.

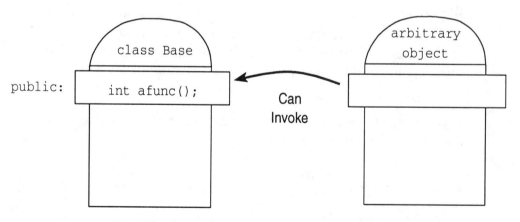

Public functions are easily invoked

You may wonder what happens if we don't use the "public" keyword when specifying member functions.

By default, a member function is private. That means that the function can only be accessed by other members of the same class.

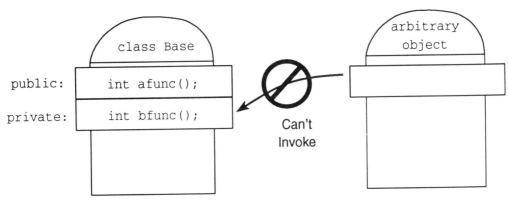

Private functions are restricted

Both of the following code examples specify private member functions:

```
class Base {
   private:
        /* ... */
};
```

or, we can use the default member access, which is "private."

```
class Base {
        /* ... */
};
```

The original version of C++ had only private and public members.

But it was quickly discovered that another level of security was needed. That is because we sometimes want derived objects to have access to functions in a base object.

With public and private, the only way to give access to a derived object is to make the function public: But a public function can be accessed by anyone. That may be a problem for some applications.

The solution was to create a new keyword which allows only the base class and derived classes to access the function. That new keyword is "protected."

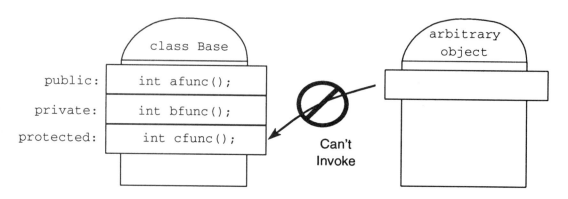

Protected Members are restricted

A class which has all three types of members could be created using:

```
class Base {
    public:
        int afunc(){};
    private:
```

```
        int bfunc() {};
    protected:
        int cfunc() {};
};
```

Although these protection mechanisms may seem straightforward, there are a large number of combinations which they may be used in.

In particular, a derived object may specify the base class as being either public or private, which can cause some confusion.

Derived Object Security

When we've created derived classes, we've always specified them as using a public base class:

```
class Derived: public Base {
    /* ... */
};
```

When an object uses a public base class, then all functions which are public in the base class are considered public in the derived class.

From the perspective of the derived class, this can be viewed as:

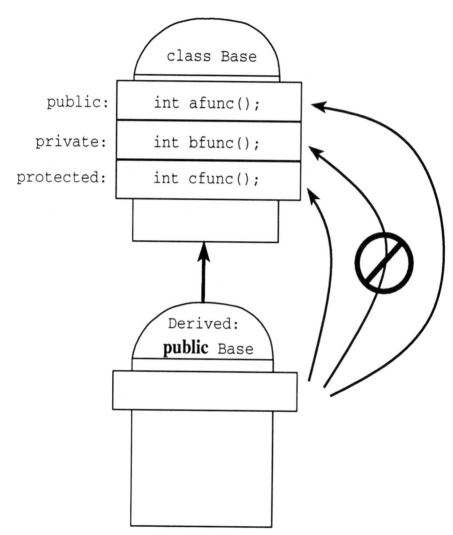

Derived Objects can't use Private Members

The alternative to using a public base class is to use a private one.

This would be specified in either of the following ways:

```
class Derived: private Base {
   /* ... */
};
```

or, one can get a private base class by using the compiler default.

```
class Derived: Base {
   /* ... */
};
```

A class which uses a private base class considers all private functions of the base class to be private to any other objects.

From the perspective of the derived object:

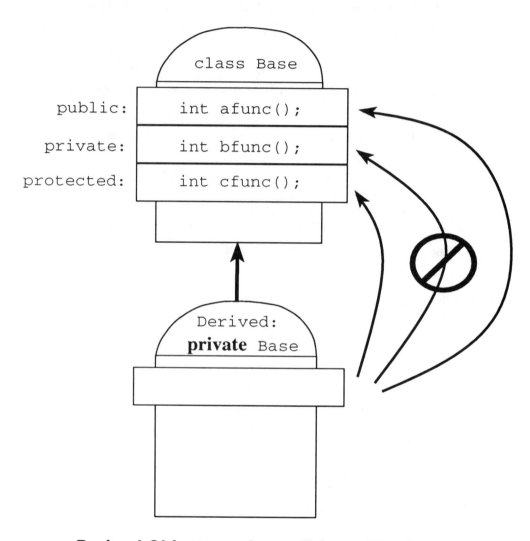

Derived Objects can't use Private Members

You may have noticed that this diagram is exactly the same as the last one. That is, to the derived object, public or private base classes are equivalent.

The difference between the two is evident to an unrelated object, however.

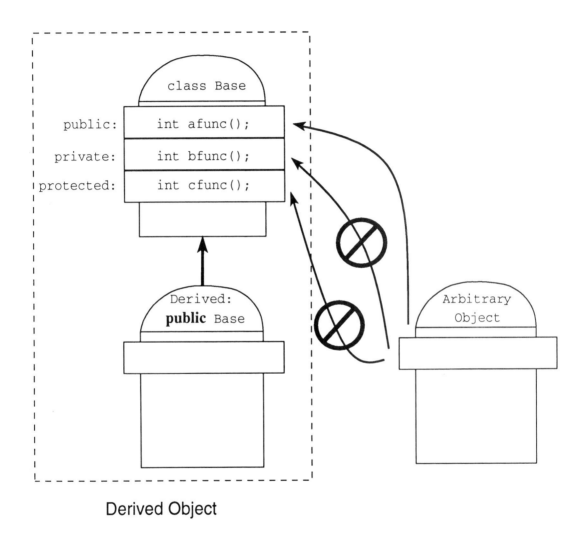

Derived Object

Other objects have restricted access

So, specifying a public base class means that you want to keep the base class's concept of public. If you had specified a private base class, then access would be even more restricted.

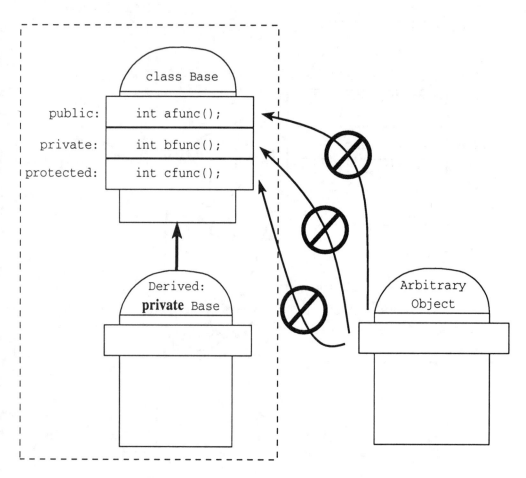

Derived Object

Private Base's are more restrictive

Most programmers avoid these problems completely by making everything public. Of course, that may be appropriate for some programs, and inappropriate for others.

If, on the other hand, you want to use the security features which C++ provides, then you will quickly discover that you also need some way to subvert those security features.

It is not unusual to have some function which needs access to the members of a class.

Those classes or functions which need unrestricted access are called "friend" functions or "friend" classes, since that is the keyword which provides access to members of a class.

Friends

So, in C++, a friend function is a function which has access to the members of a class *as though that function were a member of the class.*

```
class Base
{
     friend somefunc();
     afunc() { printf("in private function\n"); };
};


Base objB;


somefunc()
{
objB.afunc();
```

```
        }

        main(int argc, char argv[])
        {
                somefunc();
        }
```

Running this code yields:

```
        in private function
```

Further, it is possible to specify that all members of a class are friends.

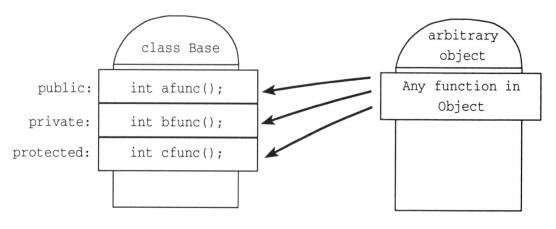

Friend of Base

Friends have unrestricted access

An example of a class which is a friend is:

```
class Base
{
   friend class arbitraryClass;
   privateFunc() { printf("in private function\n");
};
};


class arbitraryClass
{
   public:
   anyfunc(Base& objB){ objB.privateFunc(); };
};


Base objB;
arbitraryClass arb;

main(int argc, char argv[])
{
   arb.anyfunc(objB);
}
```

Runing this code yields:

```
in private function
```

So, either classes or functions may be designated as friends.

Yet, this is not the whole story.

The use of "friend" objects, in combination with "public" and "private" base classes, can lead to some complex relationships.

The following diagram illustrates the effect of a friend when using an object derived from a public base class.

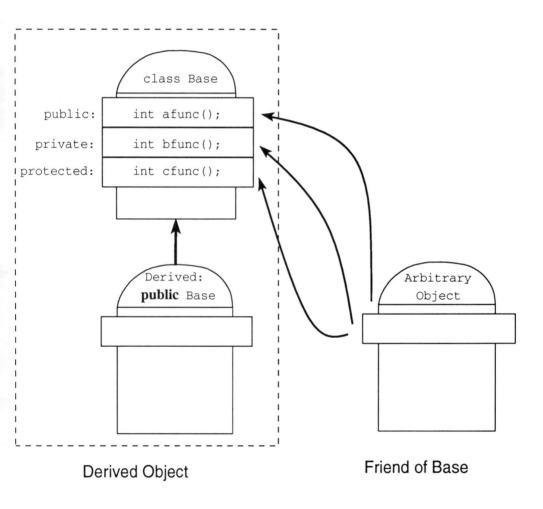

Derived Object   Friend of Base

Some code which illustrates this kind of relationship between friends is:

```
class Base
{
   friend class arbitraryClass;
   public: publicFunc(){ printf("in publicFunc\n");
};
   private: privateFunc() { printf("in
privateFunc\n"); };
   protected: protectedFunc(){ printf("in
protectedFunc\n"); };
};


class Derived:Base
{
   public: int x;
};



class arbitraryClass
{
   public:
   anyfunc(Base& objB){
      objB.privateFunc();
      objB.publicFunc();
      objB.protectedFunc();
   };
};


Derived objD;
arbitraryClass arb;
```

```
main(int argc, char argv[])
{
    arb.anyfunc(objD);
}
```

Running this code yields the expected results:

```
in privateFunc
in publicFunc
in protectedFunc
```

The other common scenarios are pictured in the diagrams which follow.

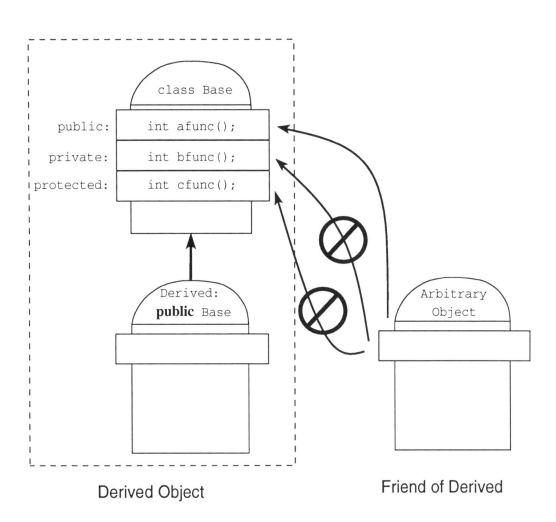

Derived Object   Friend of Derived

Protected Functions are Protected

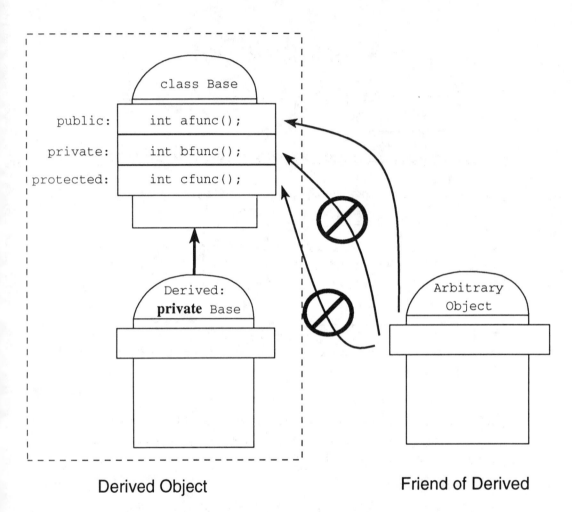

Only Access to Base's Public Members

In summary, there are really only three keywords which control access to an object. And, although those keywords are straightforward, it is the inheritance tree which will make access control non-intuitive.

Chapter Seven
C++ with X11 and NeXT

In this Chapter we will be looking at two small example programs.

In the first example we will integrate C++ with the X Window System, and in the second example we will integrate C++ with NeXT's proprietary windowing system.

The intent of these examples is not to teach either of the window systems. In fact, the intent is not to teach Object Oriented Programming, either.

Rather, the intent is to integrate the basic skills which we've acquired with C++: Skills such as the ability to use objects and virtual functions in a "real" piece of code.

This Chapter is divided into three parts: The first part describes the "generic" C++ portion of both examples. That is followed by the section with X Window System code, and then NeXT's proprietary window system code.

The Base C++ Objects

The examples we will use are built around three objects. These objects provide a core functionality which is extended in each of the examples.

C++ objects designed with virtual functions to be implemented later

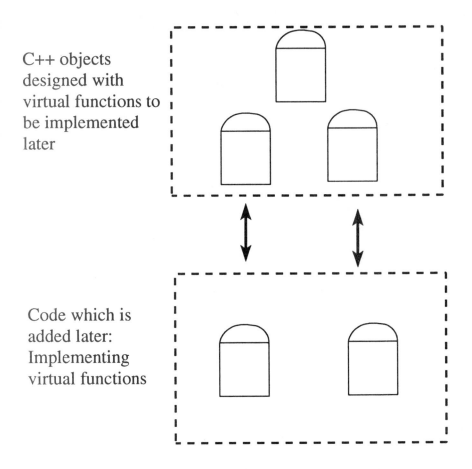

Code which is added later: Implementing virtual functions

Virtual Functions provide coupling

Using virtual functions in our objects allows us to build other code which calls those virtual functions: *We can call those functions without knowing when those virtual functions will be implemented.*

Similarly, another programmmer will be able to call our code, which uses objects of our type, *even though that programmer may be using derived objects.*

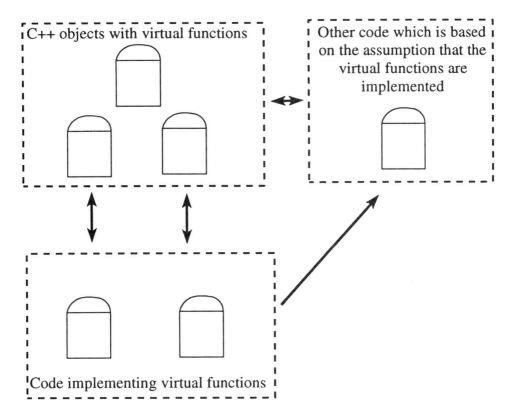

Modifications will not break dependencies

In our example, we will implement three objects: An object which has common display functions, an object which knows how to display "surfaces," and an object which knows how to display "holes."

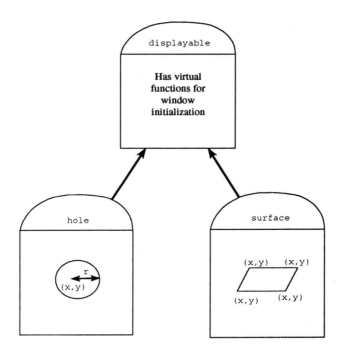

Displayable Objects use same base Object

Since our "displayable" object has common display functions, each object which may need those functions will be derived from it.

Since both the "hole" and the "surface" must know how to display themselves, and yet must be modifiable for different displays, we will make thier display methods virtual.

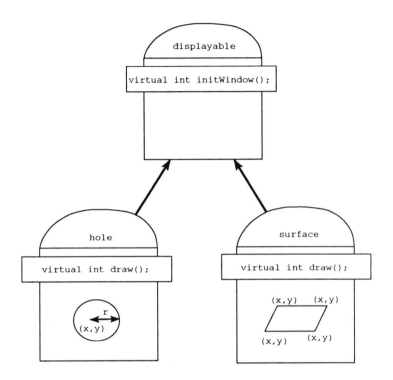

Implementation dependent code is virtual

Similarly, the "initWindow" function is virtual, since it must be modified for a particular display device.

We will also use an overloaded "+" operator, which will associate a hole with a surface. Conceptually, "+" will add a hole to a surface. Programmatically, we will add the hole to a list associated with the surface.

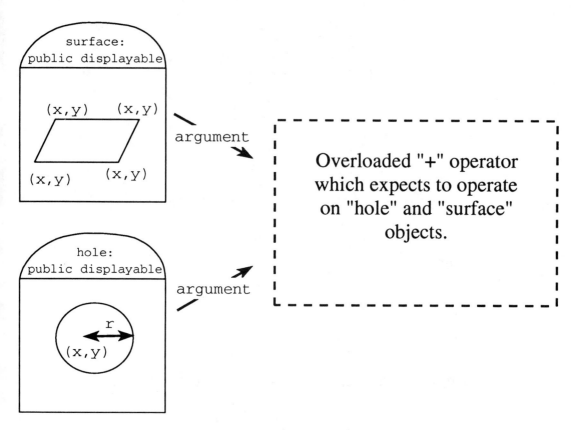

Can rely on virtual functions

We will also be able to use this overloaded operator with objects derived from "hole" and "surface." Which, in fact, *is* Object Oriented Programming: The object encapsulates knowledge of its virtual function pointers, allowing derived objects to use this overloaded operator.

Since we will be adding holes to a list associated with a surface, we will also keep an array and an index into that array.

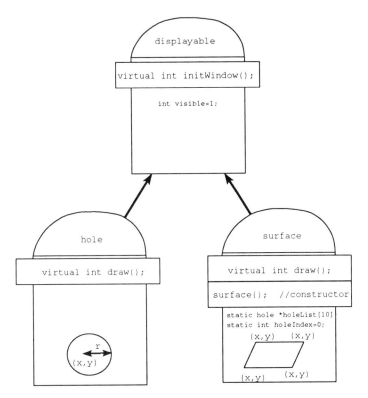

A few more details

Ok. Now we are ready for the real code.

An X Window System Example

This code will create derived objects, and then, after implementing the virtual functions, display the "surface" with "holes" in an X based window.

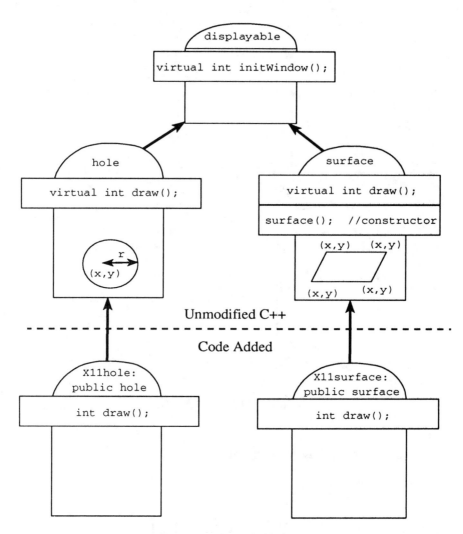

X Window Modifications

Use this line to compile the sample code:

```
cc++ -o x   x.c -lX11 -lg++
```

The code follows:

```
extern "C" { /* special C++ syntax to stop type check */
#include <stdio.h>
#include <ctype.h>
#include <signal.h>
#include <setjmp.h>
#include <assert.h>
#include <math.h>
#include </usr/include/string.h>
#include <X11/Xlib.h>
#include <X11/Xutil.h>
#include <X11/Xproto.h>
#include <X11/cursorfont.h>
#include <X11/keysym.h>
#include <X11/keysymdef.h>
}

int gargc;              /* global version of argc */
char **gargv;           /* global version of argv */

/*
 *    The following C++ is unchanged between versions
 */
class displayable {
  public:
    int visible=1;
    virtual initWindow(){};
};
```

```
class hole: public displayable {
  public:
    int radius=8;
    int xcenter=50,ycenter=50;
    virtual int draw(){};
};

class surface: public displayable {
  public:
    int x[4],y[4];        // four corners
    static hole *holeList[10];    // holes in surface
    static int holeIndex=0;    // index for above array
    surface()              // constructor
    {
    x[0]=5;y[0]=5;x[1]=5;y[1]=200;
    x[2]=200;y[2]=200;x[3]=200;y[3]=5;
    }
    virtual int draw(){};
};

void operator+(surface& s, hole& h)
{
  s.holeList[s.holeIndex++]=&h;
  if(s.visible) s.draw();
  for(int i=0; i<s.holeIndex; i++) {
    if(h.visible) s.holeList[i]->draw();
  }
}

/*
 *    Below is the interface specific code -- X windows
 */
```

```
class X11surface: public surface {
  private:
      static Display *D;
      static Window window;
      static GC theGC;
    friend class X11hole;     // so it can use window arg
  public:
      int draw();
      int initWindow();
};


X11surface::initWindow()
{
  XEvent event;
  XGCValues dummy;  /* used as a placeholder in call */
  static XSizeHints xsh = { /* hints for window mger */
      (USPosition|USSize|PPosition|PSize|PMinSize),
      10, 10,                   /* x & y coordinate */
      500,500,                /* width, height */
      300, 200                /* min width, min height */
    };
  static XWMHints xwmh = {    /* hints for window mger */
      (InputHint | StateHint),  /* flags */
      False,                    /* input */
      NormalState,              /* initial_state */
      0, 0, 0, 0, 0,  0,
    };

  assert(  ((D=XOpenDisplay(NULL)) != NULL)  );

  window = XCreateSimpleWindow(D,
          DefaultRootWindow(D), xsh.x, xsh.y,
```

```
        xsh.width, xsh.height, 2, WhitePixel(D,
              DefaultScreen(D)),
        BlackPixel(D, DefaultScreen(D)));
    assert(window);
    theGC = XCreateGC(D, window, 0, &dummy);
    XSetForeground(D, theGC, WhitePixel(D,
              DefaultScreen(D)));
    XSetStandardProperties(D, window,"Holes","Holes",
              None, gargv, gargc, &xsh);
    XSetWMHints(D, window, &xwmh);
    XSelectInput(D, window,
StructureNotifyMask|ButtonPressMask|ButtonMotionMask|B
uttonReleaseMask);
    XMapWindow(D, window);
    XFlush(D);
    do {
        XNextEvent(D, &event);
    } while (event.type != MapNotify ||
              event.xmap.window != window);


}


X11surface::draw()
{
    XDrawLine(D, window, theGC,this->x[3],
              this->y[3],this->x[0],this->y[0]);
    for(int i=0; i<3; i++) {
      XDrawLine(D, window, theGC,this->x[i],
              this->y[i],this->x[i+1],this->y[i+1]);
    }
    XFlush(X11surface::D);
}
```

```
class X11hole: public hole {
  public:
    int draw() {
      XDrawArc(X11surface::D, X11surface::window,
            X11surface::theGC,this->xcenter,
            this->ycenter,this->radius,this->radius,
            0, 360*64);
    XFlush(X11surface::D);
    }
};




main(int argc,char **argv)
{
  X11hole holeObj;
  X11surface surfaceObj;
  X11hole *aHolePtr;

   gargc=argc;     // global versions of args
   gargv=argv;

  surfaceObj.initWindow();

  // add a default hole to the surface
  (surface)surfaceObj + (hole)holeObj;

  sleep(5);    // keep on screen briefly

  // create hole object, modify it, and add to surface
  aHolePtr = new X11hole;
  aHolePtr->xcenter=75;
```

```
aHolePtr->ycenter=15;
aHolePtr->radius=5;

(surface)surfaceObj + (hole)*aHolePtr;

sleep(5); // keep on screen briefly
}
```

There is a screen dump of the output for the NeXT version of this program at the end of the NeXT section.

The output is identical except for the inverted orientation on the NeXT.

You may have noticed that this example didn't use "callbacks" to any member functions. That is because the X Window System has no concept of a pointer to a member function. In general, callbacks must be handled by a global C function which then passes control to a C++ function.

Or, alternatively, the member function can be made static, and there will then be only a single copy of the function in the program. That function can then be used in a callback.

A NeXTstep Example

This example illustrates that C++ is sufficiently flexible to deal with proprietary window systems: Even a window system which is built around a proprietary language: Objective-C.

Like the last example, we will create derived objects which implement the virtual functions, and then use them to display two holes in a surface.

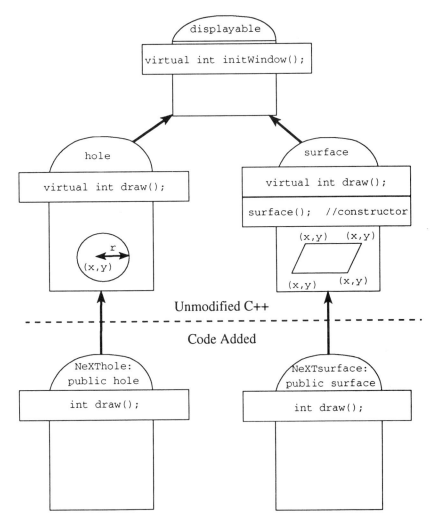

NeXT Modifications

This example was compiled on a NeXT machine using:

```
cc++ -o next next.c -lg++ -lNeXT_s
```

```
extern "Objective-C" /* Stop type checking in block */
{
#import <appkit/appkit.h>
#import <stdio.h>
#import <dpsclient/dpsNeXT.h>
#import <dpsclient/wraps.h>
#import <appkit/graphics.h>
}

/*
 *      The following C++ is unchanged between versions
 */
class displayable {
  public:
    int visible=1;
    virtual initWindow(){};
};

class hole: public displayable {
  public:
    int radius=8;
    int xcenter=50,ycenter=50;
    virtual int draw(){};
};

class surface: public displayable {
```

```
public:
  int x[4],y[4];        // four corners
  static hole *holeList[10];    // holes in surface
  static int holeIndex=0;    // index for above array
  surface()              // constructor
  {
  x[0]=5;y[0]=5;x[1]=5;y[1]=200;
  x[2]=200;y[2]=200;x[3]=200;y[3]=5;
  }
  virtual int draw(){};
};

void operator+(surface& s, hole& h)
{
  s.holeList[s.holeIndex++]=&h;
  if(s.visible) s.draw();
  for(int i=0; i<s.holeIndex; i++) {
    if(h.visible) s.holeList[i]->draw();
  }
}


/*
 * Below is the interface specific code - NeXT's
 * proprietary window system
 */
class NeXTsurface: public surface {
  private:
    static int newWindowNumber;
    static DPSContext context;
    friend class NeXThole;    // so it can use context arg
  public:
    int draw();
```

```
      int initWindow() {

         context = DPSCreateContext(NULL, NULL, NULL,
NULL);

         DPSPrintf(context,"/myWindow 10 10 500 500
Buffered window def\n");

         DPSPrintf(context,"Above 0 myWindow
orderwindow\n");

         DPSPrintf(context,"myWindow
windowdeviceround\n");

         DPSFlushContext(context);

      }

};


NeXTsurface::draw()

{

  DPSPrintf(context,"newpath\n");

  DPSPrintf(context,"%d %d moveto\n",this->x[3], this-
>y[3]);

  for(int i=0; i<4; i++) {

      DPSPrintf(context,"%d %d lineto\n",this->x[i],
this->y[i]);

      DPSPrintf(context,"stroke\n");

      DPSPrintf(context,"%d %d moveto\n",this->x[i],
this->y[i]);

  }

  DPSPrintf(context,"flushgraphics  \n");

  DPSFlushContext(context);

}


class NeXThole: public hole {

  public:

    int draw() {

      DPSPrintf(NeXTsurface::context,"newpath\n");

      DPSPrintf(NeXTsurface::context,"%d %d %d 0 360
arc\n",this->xcenter, this->ycenter,this->radius);
```

```
        DPSPrintf(NeXTsurface::context,"fill\n");

DPSPrintf(NeXTsurface::context,"flushgraphics\n");
        DPSFlushContext(NeXTsurface::context);
    }
};



main()
{
  NeXThole holeObj;
  NeXTsurface surfaceObj;
  NeXThole *aHolePtr;

  surfaceObj.initWindow();

  // add a default hole to the surface
  (surface)surfaceObj + (hole)holeObj;

  sleep(5);   // keep on screen briefly

  // create a hole object, modify it, and add to surface
  aHolePtr = new NeXThole;
  aHolePtr->xcenter=75;
  aHolePtr->ycenter=15;
  aHolePtr->radius=5;

  (surface)surfaceObj + (hole)*aHolePtr;

  sleep(5); // keep on screen briefly
}
```

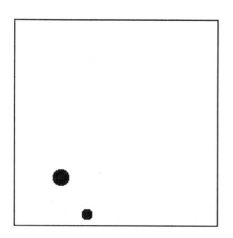

The NeXT window dump

You may have noticed that this example did not use the Application Kit, which is a set of objects based on the Objective-C language. That is because we would have had to use Objective-C in order to invoke those object: And we only now got to the point of using C++. NeXT provides the example CalculatorLab++ which uses C++ and Objective-C with thier "AppKit."

Chapter Eight
Miscellaneous Features

The C++ language sometimes seems like a collector's dream: It collects many new features, some adding little, if any, power to the language.

In this Chapter, we go over a variety of features: some of them are useful.

Input and Output

A potentially useful new feature consists of a set of objects. This set of objects is designed to replace the "stdio" library of C.

In practice, most programmers have little reason to become well acquainted with this I/O library: primarily because of the proliferation of Window Systems, which have their own I/O mechanisms.

In C++, the operator "<<" is designed to be used with the "cout" object in order to allow printing. I've compiled my small example making sure that my include files were found.

```
cc++ -o stream  stream.c -I/C++/Libg++-1.37.0 -I/C++/
Libg++-1.37.0/g++-include  -lg++
```

This code prints "Hello World" to standard out.

```
#include <stream.h>

main()
{
   cout << "Hello World\n";
}
```

Running this code produced:

```
Hello World
```

Similarly, multiple variables of different types can be output by successively invoking the overloaded "<<" operator, and taking advantage of the fact that C++ will call the correct function implementation based on argument type.

```
#include <stream.h>

main()
{
   int x=5;
   char y[]="abc";
   cout << y << x;
}
```

Running this code produced:

```
abc5
```

There is a "special" technique to flush the buffered output queue, and that is to use the word "flush" in your output statement.

```
cout << y << x << flush;
```

Input is done with the `cin` operator. Something like this:

```
int x;
cin >> x;
```

Since cin and cout are really objects, which have a heirarchy associated with them, they have much more functionality than we are examining. My terse treatment of them assumes that you will probably be programming with some higher level I/O system.

Function Prototypes

The C++ language does extensive type checking. In order for it to perform that type checking, it must know the argument types for functions. Therefore, function prototypes are required.

A typical prototype might have this form:

```
float myfunc(int x, float y);
```

The argument names are not necessary, and the variable type alone would be sufficient.

Function Defaults

It is possible to specify default arguments for functions.

void

myfunc(int x, char ch='a')

{

/* ... */

}

In this case, the function myfunc can be invoked with either one or two arguments. If it is invoked with one argument, the second argument will use the default value.

Defaults can be specified only for the "trailing" arguments.

That is, this is permissible:

```
myfunc(int x, char ch='a', int y=10);
```

while this is not permissible:

```
myfunc(int x=5, char ch, int y=10);
```

Functions with a variable number of args

Since all functions require prototypes, what happens to a function which takes a variable number of arguments? The answer is illustrated by this line of code:

```
int printf(char * ... );
```

Inline Functions

Many compilers support the "inlining" of functions: That is, they replicate the code at each place the function is invoked.

C++ supports this feature in the language definition.

```
inline afunc(int x)
{
   x = x & 0x00ff;
}
```

Many new programmers go to great effort to minimize function calls. And, perhaps, on very old machines that would help.

But most modern processors assume that a multitasking operating system will be used; and that function calls should, by their nature, be an efficient operation.

It is rare that function calls are a bottleneck in programs: It is better to become acquainted with the profiling tools of your system, and optimize where it may actually help performance.

Block Scoped Declarations

It is possible create variables which are local to their block. The most common use of this feature looks like:

```
for(int x=0; x<10; x++) {
 /* ... */
}
```

The "const" keyword

It is possible in C++ to define variables which cannot be changed: These are called "const."

They cannot be assigned to, and they must be initialized.

Two examples of it's use are:

```
const int x=50;
const char *ptr="abc" /* constant string */
```

It is worth noticing that the second example makes the string a constant. A constant pointer would use the operator "*const".

```
char *const ptr ="abc" /* constant pointer */
```

Unions

A feature which adds no functionality, yet is hard to dislike, is the ability to ignore the naming of unions.

These are sometimes called "anonymous unions".

```
struct aStruct {
  union {      // unnamed
     int aMember;
     int anotherMember;
  };
};

main()
{
struct aStruct st;
st.aMember;    // no union name required
}
```

Of course, in traditional C we would have given the union a name and used it to access the members of the union.

Structures are Types

Structures are automatically considered a type, so the code above did not need to say:

```
struct aStruct st;
```

and could have been written like this:

```
struct aStruct {
  union {        // unnamed
      int aMember;
      int anotherMember;
   };
};

main()
{
aStruct st;
st.aMember;      // no union name required
}
```

Enumeration

It is possible to automatically create constants and assign them values.

The long form of doing this would be:

```
const int FRONT=0;
const int BACK=1;
```

The short form, which uses enumeration, looks like:

```
enum side {FRONT,BACK} ;

main()
{
side x;
}
```

This is most useful as a form of "commenting" code.

Comments

As has been used in many examples in this book, the "//" indicates that the remainder of the line is a comment.

This is most useful when commenting the body of functions, since the entire function can then be commented out with the "/*" and the "*/".

```
// I am a comment to the end of the line
```

Void

There is a type void, which is not any type.

It is most useful because some routines simply work with void pointers: passing them in and out. The calling functions know their type, and use them appropriately.

While it is possible to have functions of type void, it is not possible to have objects of type void.

Casting

There is an alternative to the traditional technique of casting. Rather than use:

```
(int) myptr;
```

This can be used instead:

```
int (myptr);
```

Disabling Type Checking

Type checking can be disabled in a block by enclosing it with:

```
extern "C"
{
   /* no type checking in here */
}
```

Of course, this technique is quite popular when porting C code to

C++, since existing C code does not usually do the level of type checking required by C++.

Some other implementation allow:

```
extern "someUniqueString"
{
}
```

In order to tell the compiler that it will encounter some non-C++ syntax in the block. Of course, this is compiler dependent.

Chapter Eight

Appendix
Getting Free C++

In the economic world, there are two types: The "haves," and the "have-nots."

In the world of programmers, we have the same concept: Those programmers who have access to the Internet, and those programmers who do not have access to the Internet.

The analogy is quite accurate. In both cases, those with resources, whether they are source code or money, are able to do more things. Those without resources are not ready when an opportunity arises.

If you have access to the Internet, then it is possible to easily download all the sources to GNU's version of C++.

If you don't have access to the Internet, then we have to do one of:

1) Get access to the Internet

2) Set up a uucp communication link

3) Pay money to get a source tape using US Mail.

We will start out assuming that you have access to the Internet, and download a file which describes how to download source files from the internet..

Ordering via mail will be described next, followed by paid access.

Where are the archive sites?

If you have Internet access, then the "ftp" utility can be used to download the sources from any of several sites.

Although the list of sites which have the sources can change, this is accurate as of the beginning of 1991.

a.cs.uiuc.edu	128.174.252.1	TeX, dvi2ps, gif, texx2.7,
a.cs.uiuc.edu		amiga, GNUmake, GNU
addvax.llnl.gov	128.115.19.32	GNU Emacs
aeneas.mit.edu	18.71.0.38	GNU emacs, kerberos
ames.arc.nasa.gov	128.102.18.3	pcrrn, GNU grep, conf, grep,
ccb.ucsf.edu	128.218.1.13	comp.sources, GNU stuff,
ccb.ucsf.edu		sound_list archives
cs.uni-sb.de	134.96.7.254	GNU, atari, RFCs, perl, misc
cs.uni-sb.de		utils
dept.csci.unt.edu	129.120.1.2	Texas Packet Radio Society,
dept.csci.unt.edu		MixView, GNUPlot
dg-rtp.dg.com	128.222.1.2	GDB, DG version of GNU C for
dg-rtp.dg.com		88K
hobiecat.cs.caltech.edu	131.215.131.167	GNU
hp4nl.nluug.nl	192.16.202.2	GNU, ABC
hpcvaaz.cv.hp.com	15.255.72.15	MitX11R4 Motif

hurratio.tde.lth.se	130.235.32.22	GNU stuff, some local elisp
hurratio.tde.lth.se		stuff
hydra.helsinki.fi	128.214.4.29	misc, TeX, X,
hydra.helsinki.fi		comp.sources.misc,
hydra.helsinki.fi		comp.sources.sun,
hydra.helsinki.fi		comp.sources.unix,
hydra.helsinki.fi		comp.bugs.4bsd.ucb-fixes,
hydra.helsinki.fi		comp.binaries.ibm.pc
iamsun.unibe.ch	130.92.64.10	ET++, GNU, graphics stuff
isdres.er.usgs.gov	130.11.48.2	US Geological Survey Maps
isy.liu.se	130.236.1.3	GNU stuff, screen 2.0, world
isy.liu.se		map, ccmd, ftpd, TIFF
isy.liu.se		library, Cellsim
itnsg1.cineca.it	130.186.1.194	NCSA software, Silcon
itnsg1.cineca.it		Graphics, Graphics and
itnsg1.cineca.it		Visualization, Unix
j.cc.purdue.edu	128.210.5.1	comp.sources.unix,
j.cc.purdue.edu	128.210.9.2	comp.sources.x,
j.cc.purdue.edu		comp.sources.amiga, elm,
j.cc.purdue.edu		uupc, comp.binaries.amiga,
j.cc.purdue.edu		comp.sources.sun
jaguar.utah.edu	128.110.4.71	GNU
kampi.hut.fi	130.233.224.2	DES routines (unrestricted),
kampi.hut.fi		GNU pascal
kappa.rice.edu	128.42.4.7	X11R3, GNU for Sequent S27,
kappa.rice.edu		Sun3

labrea.stanford.edu	36.8.0.47	GNU, X, official TeX sources,
labrea.stanford.edu		lots of other stuff
larry.mcrcim.mcgill.edu	132.206.1.1	RFCs, X, local nameserver,
larry.mcrcim.mcgill.edu	132.206.4.3	games, scred (sun bitmap
larry.mcrcim.mcgill.edu		editor)
latour.colorado.edu	128.138.204.19	resource discovery papers
lcs.mit.edu	18.26.0.36	RFCs, Map, telecom archive
maccs.dcss.mcmaster.ca	130.113.1.1	GNU, fbm, pbmplus, sun fixes
nic.funet.fi	128.214.6.100	GNU, X11, networking, msdos,
nic.funet.fi		mac, amiga, atari, security
nic.funet.fi		docs and software,
nic.funet.fi		cryptography stuff, sony news
nic.funet.fi		software
oswego.oswego.edu	129.3.1.1	GNU, mac, kermit
qed.rice.edu	128.42.4.38	GNU, X11R3, plot2ps sources
schizo.samsung.com	134.228.1.2	alt.sources,
schizo.samsung.com		comp.sources.games,
schizo.samsung.com		comp.sources.misc,
schizo.samsung.com		comp.sources.sun,
schizo.samsung.com		comp.sources.unix,
schizo.samsung.com		comp.sources.x, GNU, usenet
schizo.samsung.com		news sw, unix mail sw,
schizo.samsung.com		networking sw, msdos, gifs,
schizo.samsung.com		RFCs
sun.cnuce.cnr.it	192.12.192.4	atalk, ka9q, GNU
sun.soe.clarkson.edu	128.153.12.3	Packet Driver, X11 fonts,

sun.soe.clarkson.edu		TeX, PCIP, Freemacs, LaTeX
sun.soe.clarkson.edu		styles
trout.nosc.mil	128.49.16.7	X11R3, benchmarks, popd, GNU
trout.nosc.mil	132.249.16.12	emacs
unicorn.cc.wwu.edu	140.160.240.10	GNU dbm
unix.secs.oakland.edu	141.210.180.2	gcc, gas, gdb, and kermit for
unix.secs.oakland.edu		xenix
uxc.cso.uiuc.edu	128.174.5.50	games, HitchHiker's Guide to
uxc.cso.uiuc.edu		the Internet, recipes, GIF,
uxc.cso.uiuc.edu		GNU, RFC, IEN, and more
watmsg.waterloo.edu	129.97.129.9	GNU, pd BSD, uSystem docs,
watmsg.waterloo.edu		virus, cryptography
wuarchive.wustl.edu RFCs,	128.252.135.4	GNU, X.11R3, GIF, IEN,
wuarchive.wustl.edu		TeX, UUPC, info-mac,
wuarchive.wustl.edu		4.3BSD-Tahoe,
wuarchive.wustl.edu		comp.binaries.amiga,
wuarchive.wustl.edu		comp.binaries.apple2,
wuarchive.wustl.edu		comp.binaries.atari.st,
wuarchive.wustl.edu		comp.binaries.ibm.pc,
wuarchive.wustl.edu		comp.sources.amiga,
wuarchive.wustl.edu		comp.sources.atari.st,
wuarchive.wustl.edu		comp.sources.games,
wuarchive.wustl.edu		comp.sources.misc,
wuarchive.wustl.edu		comp.sources.sun,
wuarchive.wustl.edu		comp.sources.unix,
wuarchive.wustl.edu		comp.sources.x, msdos,

wuarchive.wustl.edu   simtel20, elm (24 hours/day)

We will go through a sample session using "ftp" to access the sources on "prep.ai.mit.edu." This is done from a UNIX machine, and I will use the login name "anonymous" and give a password which is my Internet mailing address (which is not echoed in the script below)

```
$ ftp prep.ai.mit.edu
Connected to prep.ai.mit.edu.
220 aeneas FTP server (Version 4.136 Mon Oct 31 23:18:38
EST 1988) ready.
Name (prep.ai.mit.edu:ann): anonymous
331 Guest login ok, send ident as password.
Password:
230 Guest login ok, access restrictions apply.
ftp> cd pub/gnu
250 CWD command successful.
ftp> get GETTING.GNU.SOFTWARE
200 PORT command successful.
150 Opening data connection for GETTING.GNU.SOFTWARE
(129.18.2.14,3415) (3311 bytes).
226 Transfer complete.
local: GETTING.GNU.SOFTWARE remote: GETTING.GNU.SOFTWARE
3395 bytes received in 0.44 seconds (7.57 Kbytes/s)
ftp> quit
221 Goodbye.
$
```

Rather than trying to paraphrase the real instructions, the file is printed below:

-*- text -*-

Getting GNU Software, 19 Sep 90

Copyright (C) 1986, 1987, 1988, 1989, 1990 Free Software Foundation, Inc.

Permission is granted to anyone to make or distribute
verbatim copies of this document provided that the
copyright notice and this permission notice are preserved.

* GNU and the Free Software Foundation

Project GNU is organized as part of the Free Software Foundation, Inc.
The Free Software Foundation has the following goals:
 1) to create GNU as a full development/operating system.
 2) to distribute GNU and other useful software with source code and
permission to copy and redistribute.

Further information on the rationale for GNU is in file
/pub/gnu/etc/GNU (All files referred to are on the Internet host
prep.ai.mit.edu.

Information on GNU Internet mailing lists and gnUSENET newsgroupscan
be found in file /pub/gnu/etc/MAILINGLISTS.

* How To Get The Software

The easiest way to get a copy of the distribution is from someone else who has it. You need not ask for permission to do so, or tell any one else; just copy it. The second easiest is to ftp it over the Internet. The third easiest way is to uucp it. Ftp and uucp information is in file /pub/gnu/etc/FTP.

If you cannot get a copy any of these ways, or if you would feel more confident getting copies straight from us, or if you would like to get some funds to us to help in our efforts, you can order one from the Free Software Foundation. See file /pub/gnu/etc/DISTRIB.

* Available Software

** GNU Emacs

The GNU Emacs distribution includes:
- manual source in TeX format.
- an enhanced regex (regular expression) library.

See file /pub/gnu/etc/MACHINES for the status of porting Emacs to various machines and operating systems.

** C Scheme - a block structured dialect of LISP.

The Free Software Foundation distributes C Scheme for the MIT Scheme

Project on it tapes. A partial ftp distribution can be found on prep.ai.mit.edu. The full ftp distribution can be found on zurich.ai.mit.edu.

Problems with the C Scheme distribution and it's ftp distribution should be referred to: <bug-cscheme@prep.ai.mit.edu>. There are two general mailing lists: <scheme@mc.lcs.mit.edu> and <info-cscheme@prep.ai.mit.edu>. Requests to join either list to: <info-cscheme-request@prep.ai.mit.edu> or <scheme-request@mc.lcs.mit.edu>.

** Other GNU Software

A fuller list of available software are in the files /pub/gnu/etc/DISTRIB and /pub/gnu/etc/FTP.

* No Warranties

We distribute software in the hope that it will be useful, but without any warranty. No author or distributor of this software accepts responsibility to anyone for the consequences of using it or for whether it serves any particular purpose or works at all, unless he says so in writing.

* If You Like The Software

If you like the software developed and distributed by the Free
Software Foundation, please express your satisfaction with a donation.
Your donations will help to support the foundation and make our future
efforts successful, including a complete development and operating
system, called GNU (Gnu's Not Un*x), which will run Un*x user
programs. For more information on GNU and the Foundation, contact us
at Internet address <gnu@prep.ai.mit.edu> or the foundation's US Mail
address found in file /pub/gnu/etc/DISTRIB.

The Instructions for downloading

A session which gets the files containing instructions is shown.

```
$ ftp prep.ai.mit.edu
Connected to prep.ai.mit.edu.
220 aeneas FTP server (Version 4.136 Mon Oct 31 23:18:38
EST 1988) ready.
Name (prep.ai.mit.edu:ann): anonymous
331 Guest login ok, send ident as password.
Password:
230 Guest login ok, access restrictions apply.
ftp> cd pub/gnu/etc
250 CWD command successful.
ftp> get FTP
200 PORT command successful.
150 Opening data connection for FTP (129.18.2.14,3405)
(11748 bytes).
226 Transfer complete.
local: FTP remote: FTP
```

```
12018 bytes received in 0.78 seconds (15 Kbytes/s)
ftp> get DISTRIB
200 PORT command successful.
150 Opening data connection for DISTRIB (129.18.2.14,3406)
(13909 bytes).
226 Transfer complete.
local: DISTRIB remote: DISTRIB
14264 bytes received in 0.88 seconds (15.9 Kbytes/s)
ftp> quit
221 Goodbye.
$
```

At this point, it is a matter of following the instructions in the file. If you have no ftp access, and want to use US Mail, and are willing to pay for the reproduction, shipping, and other fees, then the following "excerpt" on ordering is important to you.

Free Software Foundation Order Form

This order form is effective June 1, 1991 - February 1, 1992

Prices and contents may change without notice.

Please allow six weeks for delivery (though it won't usually take that long).

All software and publications are distributed with permission to copy and to redistribute.

TeX source for each manual is on the appropriate tape; the prices for tapes do not include printed manuals.

All software and documentation from the Free Software Foundation is provided on an "as is" basis, with no warranty of any kind.

Quantity Price Item

For Unix systems, on 1600 bpi 9-track tape in Unix tar format:

_____ $200GNU Emacs source code and other software.
   The tape includes:
   * GNU Emacs (the extensible, customizable, self-documenting
     real-time display editor)
   * The GNU Emacs Lisp Reference Manual, as Texinfo source.
   * GDB (The GNU source-level C debugger)
   * MIT Scheme (a dialect of Lisp)
   * T, Yale's implementation of Scheme
   * Nethack (a rogue-like game)
   * GNU Chess (a chess playing program with an interface to X)
   * texi2roff (for printing Texinfo source with [nt]roff)
   * Data Compression Software (to uncompress source on the tape).

_____ $200GNU Compiler source code and related software,
   for Unix systems. The tape includes:

* GCC (the GNU C Compiler, including COFF support)

* Bison (a free, compatible replacement for yacc)

* gperf (a perfect hash-table generator)

* G++ (the C++ front end to GCC)

* lib-g++ (the G++ class library)

* NIH Class Library (formerly known as OOPS)

* Gas (the GNU Assembler)

* GNU object file utilities (ar, ld, make, gprof, size, nm,

  strip, ranlib, et al.)

* dld (a dynamic linker)

* COFF support for GNU software tools

* Groff (GNU troff and related programs)

* GDB (The GNU source-level C debugger)

* GNU make

* Bash (GNU's Bourne Again SHell)

* Gawk (the GNU implementation of the AWK programming language)

* Flex (Vern Paxson fast rewrite of lex)

* GNU tar

* the freed files from the 4.3BSD-Tahoe distribution

* RCS (Revision Control System)

* CVS (Concurrent Control System)

* GNU diff and grep

* Ghostscript (a Postscript interpreter)

* Gnuplot (an interactive mathematical plotting program)

* Perl (a programming language interpreter)

* f2c (a FORTRAN to C translator)

* gdbm library
* other GNU utilities (file utilities, indent, et al.)
* GNU GO (the GNU implementation of the game of GO)
* texi2roff (for printing Texinfo source with [nt]roff)
* Data Compression Software (to uncompress source on the tape).

_____ $200Required MIT X Window System X11R4, core software and

documentation, and contributed client software.

_____ $200 Optional MIT X Window System X11R4, contributed software

including libraries, games, Andrew and toolkits.

For Suns and other Unix Systems, on QIC-24 DC300XLP 1/4 inch cartridge tape, Unix tar format:

_____ $210 GNU Emacs and other software, as above.

_____ $210GNU compiler tape, as above.

_____ $210Required MIT X Window System X11R4, as above.

_____ $210 Optional MIT X Window System X11R4, as above.

For HP Systems, on 16-track DC600HC 1/4 inch cartridge tape, Unix tar format:

_____ $230   GNU Emacs and other software, as above.

_____ $230GNU compiler tape, as above.

_____ $230Required MIT X Window System X11R4, as above.

_____ $230   Optional MIT X Window System X11R4, as above.

For IBM RS/6000 Systems, on DC600A 1/4 inch cartridge tape Unix tar format:

_____ $215   GNU Emacs and other software, as above.
   plus executable files of Emacs.

For VMS systems, on 1600 bpi reel-to-reel 9-track tape in VMS BACKUP (aka interchange format):

_____ $195GNU Emacs source code and binaries.

_____ $195GNU C compiler source code and binaries
   Includes Bison and GAS.

GNU Emacs manual, ~300 pages, phototypeset, offset printed, spiral bound, with a reference card.

_____ $20GNU Emacs manual, unit price for 1 to 5 copies.

_____ $13GNU Emacs manuals, unit price for 6 or more.

GNU Emacs Lisp Reference Manual, ~550 pages, offset printed, spiral bound.

_____ $50   A single GNU Emacs Lisp Reference Manual.

_____ $200   Box of 5 GNU Emacs Lisp Reference Manuals.

The following documentation:

_____ $1One GNU Emacs reference card, without the manual.

_____ $5   Packet of ten GNU Emacs reference cards.

_____ $10   GDB Manual, ~70 pages, side stapled.

_____ $15Texinfo Manual, ~200 pages, spiral bound.   Texinfo is GNU's

structured documentation system, included with GNU Emacs.
Texinfo is used to produce both on-line and printed documents.
This manual describes how to write Texinfo documents.

_____ $10   Termcap Manual, ~60 pages, side stapled.   Documents the
termcap library and GNU's extensions to it.   The GNU termcap

library is included with GNU Emacs.

_____ $10   Bison Manual, ~90 pages, side stapled.

_____ $15   Gawk Manual, ~150 pages, spiral bound.

_____ $15   Make Manual, ~120 pages, spiral bound.

_____ Sub Total

_____In Massachusetts: add 5% sales tax, or give tax exempt number.

We pay for shipping via UPS ground transportation in the contiguous 48 states and Canada.

_____   In Alaska, Hawaii, or Puerto Rico, for shipping:
  - For Emacs Lisp Reference manuals, add $5 each,
    or $20 per box. For all other items, add $5 base charge,
    then $1 per item except Emacs reference cards.
If outside of U.S., Canada and Puerto Rico, for shipping costs:
  - for tapes or unboxed manuals, please add $15 base
    charge, and then add $15 more for each tape or unboxed
    manual (not reference cards) in the order:
_____   Shipping cost for tapes and unboxed manuals = $15 + $15 * n;
  - for each box of Emacs Lisp Reference manuals,

_____ please add $70.

_____ Optional tax deductible donation.

_____ Total paid

Orders are filled upon receipt of check or money order. We do not have the staff to handle the billing of unpaid orders. Please help keep our lives simple by including your payment with your order.

Please make checks payable to: "Free Software Foundation".

Please mail orders to:

Free Software Foundation, Inc.
675 Massachusetts Avenue
Cambridge, MA 02139, USA

+1 617-876-3296

This Order Form is EFFECTIVE June 1, 1991 - February 1, 1992

Name:

Mail Stop/Dept. Name

Organization:

Street Address:

City / State / Province:

Zip Code / Postal Code /Country:

In case of a problem with your order, or for overseas customs agents,
please add your voice telephone number (not your FAX's number):

For orders outside the US: Orders MUST be paid in US dollars. You are responsible for paying all duties, tariffs, and taxes. If you refuse to pay the charges, the shipper will return or abandon your order.

Please write the telephone number that you want custom agents to call in the space provided above.

This Order Form is EFFECTIVE June 1, 1991 - February 1, 1992

If you can set up UUCP

If you don't want to pay for the US Mail versions, it is also possible to get versions via uucp. The following is a reproduction of a file from Ohio State University.

This file (osu-cis!~/gnu/GNU.how-to-get) describes how to get the following software from osu-cis via semi-anonymous UUCP:

C++ Test SuiteCompressDeliver 2.0GNU Binary Utilities

GNU Assembler GNU AwkGNU BashGNU Bison

GNU C++ CompilerGNU C++ LibraryGNU C CompilerGNU Chess

GNU COFF SupportGNU CPIOGNU DBMGNU DebuggerGNU Diff

GNU Dld   GNU EmacsGNU Emacs Ada supportGNU Emacs Franz interface

GNU Emacs Lisp ManualGNU File UtilsGNU FindGNU Finger

GNU GoGNU Gperf & CperfGNU Graphics

GNU GrepGNU IndentGNU LexGNU M4

GNU MakeGNU Pins & ArtGNU Plot & Plot2PSGNU RoffGNU Sed

GNU ShellutilsGNU TarGNU TputGNUS

GhostscriptGnewsIspellKA9QM3

MIT C SchemeMg2aNNTPNewsOleoOopsPCRRN

Patch & GNU PatchPathaliasPostgresProtoize

Proxy ARPRCSRFCs & IDEASRNSB Prolog

STDWINSendmailSmail

SmalltalkVM

There's a lot of other available miscellany that isn't explicitly
listed here. You can find out about it in the file osu-cis!~/ls-lR.Z

The Computer and Information Science Department of the Ohio State
University provides Free Software Foundation GNU products (and others)
via UUCP only as a redistribution service. Anything found here is
only and exactly as it would be found on the indicated Internet hosts,
were one to acquire it via anonymous FTP (like we did); or else saved
it as it flowed past on the Usenet source distribution newsgroups.
OSU CIS takes no responsibility for the contents of any of the
distributions described in this message. See the Distribution
document (emacs/etc/DISTRIB when you unpack and build Emacs) and the
GNU Emacs General Public License (emacs/etc/COPYING, similarly).

Much of the GNU software is in beta-test. For a list of the current

statuses (stati?), ask gnu@prep.ai.mit.edu for a copy of the latest
FSF order form.

How to reach osu-cis via uucp

================================

Here is a set of L.sys or Systems file lines suitable for osu-cis:

```
#
# Direct Trailblazer
# dead, dead, dead...sigh.  for the 3rd time in as many months.
#
#osu-cis Any ACU 19200 1-614-292-5112 in:--in:--in: Uanon
#
# Direct V.32 (MNP 4)
# dead, dead, dead...sigh.
#
#osu-cis Any ACU 9600 1-614-292-1153 in:--in:--in: Uanon
#
# Micom port selector, at 1200, 2400, or 9600 bps.
# Replace ##'s below with 12, 24, or 96 (both speed and phone number).
# Can't use MNP with V.32 on -3196
#
osu-cis Any ACU ##00 1-614-292-31## "" \r\c Name? osu-cis nected \c GO
\d\r\d\r\d\r\d\r\d\r\d\r\d\r in:--in:--in: Uanon
```

Modify as appropriate for your site, of course, to deal with your
local telephone system. There are no limitations concerning the hours

of the day you may call. Note well that you cannot use MNP on the -3196 number.

We are deeply grateful to Philips Components of Eindhoven, the Netherlands for the donation of a Trailblazer Plus and a Codex 2264 for use by the community at large.

Where the files are

====================

Most items exist on osu-cis for distribution purposes in compressed tar form, exactly what you find on the indicated hosts in the specified origin files. Most items are cut into pieces for the sake of uucp sanity. This separation helps if your uucp session fails midway through a conversation; you need restart only with the part that failed, rather than the whole beast. The pieces are typically named with a root word, followed by letter pairs like "aa" and "bj," meaning that the pieces are all named with the root word, followed by a dash and the suffixes indicated, using the letters inclusive between the two limits. All pieces but the last are 100,000 bytes long, and the fragmentary last piece has some smaller size.

Other files:

  README3,970 bytes
  Release-1.5.ps.Z90,893 bytes

Report.ps.Z-part-??, pieces aa-ab [2 pieces]. part ab is 45,366 bytes.

README is the message that was posted by DEC announcing the 1.5 release. It describes briefly what Modula 3 is and the particular files are.

< descriptions of files cut from here -- Ann Weintz >

=======================
Pick a night when you can afford to be at the office late. {:-)}

Arrange to have the files uucp'd to your site. Copying the complete set of Emacs slices will take on the order of 5 hours at 2400 bps, correspondingly more at 1200. Your mileage will definitely vary, by as much as 20% on either side of that (intentionally vague) estimate. By way of comparison, a transfer of Emacs 18.50 at 2400bps to Portland, Oregon was reported to cost about $42.00, weekend rates.

NOTE: Do not request the files to be transferred using a command like

% uucp osu-cis!~/gnu/emacs/18.56/emacs* /some/local/directory

because that won't work. That will queue up a short request via *uux* to run a uucp command on osu-cis; it will fail for security reasons. You must issue many uucp commands: one for each file in each distribution you want, plus one for each diff file you want. They will all get queued and executed in as few UUCP connections as possible.

After the files have all showed up, you should extract the full distribution of GNU Emacs thusly:

cat emacs-18.57.tar.Z-part-?? | zcat | tar xvf -

Voila`, you have GNU Emacs, ready to build and cause you both joy and pain for the rest of your life. The other stuff available here is unpacked similarly.

The `zcat' mentioned above is part of the `compress' distribution, which you will have to get if you don't have it yet. Everything that we distribute (except `compress' itself) is compressed with a 16-bit Lempel-Ziv scheme. Some computers (notably those based on Intel family microprocessors) are unable for memory segmentation reasons to handle compression with a scheme higher than 12 bits. Since we can't afford the space and time to provide both 12- and 16-bit distributions via this mechanism, if you need things in a 12-bit compression format, you will need to find a cooperative friend with a full 32-bit machine to uncompress the distribution, and possibly recompress it for you in 12-bit format.

Miscellany
==========

This file of instructions exists as the file ~/GNU.how-to-get, and is updated as new distributions and diffs come out and are made available. This happens much more frequently than the full set of instructions are posted to comp.sources.d, so get it first to be sure what you are getting later in each night's UUCP transfer. Unfortunately, the worst case might be that (e.g.) if you only get part of a full distribution one night and a new version arrives during the day, you might get some of the part-*s for the old version and not know that the rest of your part-*s are from the new one. Get this file to be sure.

There's another file called ~/ls-lR.Z that contains the output of executing the comand `ls -lR' at the top level of the UUCP distribution tree. Lots of other stuff is available besides the most popular stuff that's listed here. That file is updated daily at around 3:00am Eastern time, so you may want to get it occasionally to keep up to date.

People often have problems with uucp. Feel free to write us some mail as uucp@cis.ohio-state.edu or osu-cis!uucp; we'll be happy to help as much as we can, though that is usually limited by distance and mail turnaround time.

Cheers...
Local Variables:
mode: Text
End:

If you are willing to buy Internet access

There are service organizations which will sell you access to the Internet. They usually charge a monthly fee for this "IP" service. One of these is:

UUNET Communication Service

Suite 570

3110 Fairview Park Dr.

Falls Church, VA. 22042

1 703 876 5050

I believe there is also an organization called PORTAL in Cupertino, CA, and an organization called "Performance Systems International" in Virginia which provide Internet access. Since UUNET has a reputation for apathy, you may find the others worth searching out.